Winning Design!

LEGO MINDSTORMS NXT Design Patterns for Fun and Competition

James J. Trobaugh

Apress®

Winning Design! LEGO MINDSTORMS NXT Design Patterns for Fun and Competition

ISBN-13 (pbk): 978-1-4302-2964-3

ISBN-13 (electronic): 978-1-4302-2965-0

Printed and bound in the United States of America 9 8 7 6 5 4 3 2 1

President and Publisher: Paul Manning
Lead Editor: Jonathan Gennick
Technical Reviewer: Joni Flynn
Editorial Board: Steve Anglin, Mark Beckner, Ewan Buckingham, Gary Cornell, Jonathan Gennick, Jonathan Hassell, Michelle Lowman, Matthew Moodie, Duncan Parkes, Jeffrey Pepper, Frank Pohlmann, Douglas Pundick, Ben Renow-Clarke, Dominic Shakeshaft, Matt Wade, Tom Welsh
Coordinating Editor: Anita Castro
Copy Editor: Heather Lang
Compositor: MacPS, LLC
Indexer: John Collin
Artist: April Milne
Cover Designer: Anna Ishchenko

Distributed to the book trade worldwide by Springer Science+Business Media, LLC., 233 Spring Street, 6th Floor, New York, NY 10013. Phone 1-800-SPRINGER, fax (201) 348-4505, e-mail orders-ny@springer-sbm.com, or visit www.springeronline.com.

For information on translations, please e-mail rights@apress.com, or visit www.apress.com.

Apress and friends of ED books may be purchased in bulk for academic, corporate, or promotional use. eBook versions and licenses are also available for most titles. For more information, reference our Special Bulk Sales–eBook Licensing web page at www.apress.com/info/bulksales.

Dedicated to Liz, Ian, and Amy for their love, patience and inspiration

Contents at a Glance

Contents

About the Author

 **James J. Trobaugh** has a degree in Computer Science and has been working as a software architect for 19 years. He lives in the Atlanta, Georgia area with his wife, Liz, and their two children, Ian and Amy.

He has been involved with FIRST LEGO League since 2004 as a coach for Team Super Awesome and as a technical judge at the LEGO World Festival. He is also the FLL director of the Forsyth Alliance in Forsyth County Georgia.

James started out as a LEGO hobbyist by founding the North Georgia LEGO Train Club in 1998 and has found that LEGO robotics is a natural blending of his LEGO hobby and his day job as a software architect. The added bonus is the joy of getting to share his love of technology not only with his own children but with kids in general.

About the Technical Reviewer

 **Joni Flynn** is an avid promoter of science and technology for our youth and coaches an FLL team. Her background as a systems engineer provides her teams with technical guidance. Through the success of her teams, she understands the importance of sound technical design and programming of a robot. Contributing to this book was a great opportunity for her. She also engaged her 13-year-old son Shaun, a four-year FLL team veteran, to provide another perspective on the book.

Joni lives in Michigan's Upper Peninsula where she enjoys the many outdoor activities the area provides with her husband and three children.

Introduction

Ever since the introduction of the LEGO MINDSTORMS robotics kit in 1998, there has been a desire to explore all the possibilities of what can be done with it. Along with this desire, many different LEGO robotics competitions emerged as well. Among the most popular today is FIRST LEGO League (FLL). LEGO MINDSTORMS kits have changed considerably over the years, and the current MINDSTORMS NXT system offers an array of new functionality with improved sensors, motors, and programming abilities. For people who have been working with the MINDSTORMS system for many years, these changes have been welcome additions. However, for people new to the world of LEGO robots, things can get overwhelming very quickly.

The goal of this book is to help coaches and team members better understand what it takes to build a winning robot for competitive LEGO robotics events. Some knowledge of the LEGO MINDSTORMS system would be helpful prior to using this book. The design principles covered in this book are intended not to be strict guidelines but design foundations to help get teams to the next level of competiveness.

Over the years, I have observed that teams typically need a few years of competing before they learn all the helpful tips and tricks that are used by winning teams. With the help of this book, a team should be able to learn some of these steps earlier and use them as a foundation for creating its own winning ideas and designs.

With FLL and other LEGO robotics events, winning is not always the final goal; learning how to solve problems and overcome challenges as a team are often the desired experience to take away from the event. So even though this book is intended to help with creating a winning robot design, be sure not lose sight of what the experience is all about—learning and having fun along the way.

Four Principals of a Winning Robot

This book is broken into four major principals—design, navigation, manipulation, and organization—and each of these concepts is represented in a part of this book.

Design is the thought process that every robot team needs before the first LEGO brick is even snapped together. A winning robot team not only understands the rules but the challenge that they must tackle. Part 1, "Introduction," covers the design phase.

Navigation is the art of moving a robot successfully around the playing field, and it's explained in Part 2. As you'll learn, most robots have no trouble moving, but moving consistently at an event is what makes for a winning robot.

Manipulation is extending a simple robot into a powerful robot that can control and change its environment. Learning about how properly design attachments for your robot to meet a particular challenge can make for a winning robot, as we'll explore in Part 3.

Organization is a must for any winning team. A team that has its resources organized in an efficient fashion will find that much of the chaos at LEGO robotics event will be eliminated and allow the team to focus on winning. We'll look at successful organizational strategies in Part 4, "Programming."

Getting the Most from This Book

I hope that you and your team will read through this book and find concepts and techniques that will help you in areas that you are struggling with when working with your LEGO robot. Part of the fun of building and competing with LEGO robots is the discovery, but at the same time, nothing is more frustrating than getting yourself stuck in a corner where you feel you can't move forward.

I want the topics covered to help guide you past those moments and put you back on track to having fun and learning what it takes to build a successful, winning robot. Some of what you learn in this book will be helpful to your design. Some of what you read in this book might not apply to your situation, but I believe all of what I cover to fall within the knowledge a LEGO robot designer should posses, even if it doesn't apply to your current challenge.

Enjoy the experience; be creative, and try new things. Don't be afraid to fail. And most importantly, play well!

PART 1

■ ■ ■

Introduction

■ ■ ■

CHAPTER 1

Design Considerations

Where do you start when building a LEGO robot? I know the first thing everyone wants to do is get out the LEGO parts and start snapping them together. That's one of the great things about building with LEGO elements; it's a very free-form experience. You can sit down with a pile of bricks and just start snapping parts together.

While that is the traditional way that we've all learned to play with LEGO parts, the process is not the same when building a LEGO robot, or at least, not if you're looking to build a winning LEGO robot. A complete design process is needed before the first LEGO element is snapped together. This is one of the hardest concepts for coaches to get across to their teams.

Understanding the Rules

Among of the most import things to consider when designing your robot are the rules of the competition. This may seem obvious, but it's amazing how many events I attend where a team did not fully understand the rules of the event. Take the time to carefully read all of the rules associated with the event for which you are building your robot. Have every team member read the rules; this can be important since different people may interrupt the rules differently and can shed a perspective on the rules that someone else on the team may have missed.

With events such as FIRST LEGO League (FLL), the list of rules can be very long and boring, but it's ever so important. Besides the basic rules of FLL that define what you can or can't do in regards to your actual robot design, there will also be rules for the actual game or challenge. These, too, are very important to read and fully understand, because knowing these rules will be critical in the design process of your robot. Trying to build a robot without understanding what that robot is going to be required to do will not win you any events, unless you're just super lucky.

Be aware of updates to the rules as the event preparation season continues. With FLL, the game rules are constantly being clarified or fine-tuned, so it's a good idea to check the official rules web site for any updates on a regular basis. These refinements may be posted right up to the week of competition, and some of them could have an effect on your strategy.

Also, don't be afraid to ask questions about rules. If you have read the rules but are having trouble understanding one of them, it's OK to ask for clarification. Be sure to check the rule updates first to see if someone else has already asked the same question. Web site forums are also a good place to get clarification on game rules, but remember that the official site for the event will have the most accurate answers; don't believe everything you read on the forums. Most people giving answers on forums mean well but are not always accurate.

Knowing the FLL Robot Parts Rules

Since a great deal of the examples used in this book will focus on FLL, I wanted to briefly review the parts rules in FLL that relate to robot design. Please keep in mind that this is not the complete list of rules and that the rules could change each season. Again, be sure to read the official FLL rules from the FIRST web site before starting your robot design process.

Here are the official parts rules:

1. Everything you compete with must be made of LEGO elements in original factory condition, except LEGO string and tubing, which you may cut to length. The only exception is that you can reference a paper list to keep track of programs.

2. There are no restrictions on the quantities or sources of nonelectric LEGO elements, except that factory-made wind-up or pull-back "motors" are not allowed. Pneumatics *are* allowed.

3. The electric elements used must be the LEGO MINDSTORMS type, and the total number of electric elements you may use in one match is limited as follows:

    a. NXT controller (1)

    b. Motors (3)

    c. Touch sensors (2)

    d. Light sensors (2)

    e. Lamp (1)

    f. Ultrasonic sensor (1)

After reading these rules, you can see that beyond the electronic parts that come with the MINDSTORMS kit and a few exceptions, you are allowed to use any LEGO parts on your robot. This is an important thing to note. Many teams will restrict themselves to the parts in their LEGO MINDSTORMS kit, only to realize later that they could have included other elements as well. Those Star Wars LEGO sets you may have could also contain some parts that would be helpful to your robot design. It's always a good exercise to look at various LEGO elements beyond what they were originally used for in a kit. For example, a cape on a Harry Potter LEGO figure not only makes the figure look cool but it can also be a great light shield for a LEGO light sensor. Learn to never limit a LEGO element to just one use or purpose.

Realize that there is a large assortment of other LEGO MINDSTORM sensors available from both LEGO and other vendors, but only the ones listed previously are allowed to be used at an FLL event.

Also be aware that the retail LEGO MINDSTORMS kit 2.0 does not include the standard LEGO MINDSTORMS light sensor but instead includes a color sensor.

■ **Note** Paint, tape, glue, oil, and so on are not allowed. Also stickers are not allowed, except LEGO stickers applied per LEGO instructions.

Studying the Game Mission Rules

Every robot game is going to have either a single mission or a series of missions for the robot to complete. In FLL, each year, the game will have typically have eight to ten missions, each with a certain point values. Some missions are going to be harder than others.

Each of these missions will have rules that you are required to follow to complete the mission. Some are about triggering an event, delivering an object, or retrieving an object back to base. No matter what the mission, the rules need to be understood and closely followed to ensure that your team receives the maximum number of points for the mission. Nothing is worse than practicing all season to find out that you did not understand the mission rules correctly and your robot does not do the task correctly.

With FLL and many other robotics competitions, the missions will have videos along with the written rules that help explain the goal of the mission. When watching the videos, don't let the actions you see in the video lock you into a single way of solving the mission. Many teams will see the video example and think that the example shown is the only way to complete the mission. Always read the rules and watch the videos with an open mind.

For example, in the FLL 2008 Climate Connections season, one of the missions was to deliver some items over an arctic ice bearer. Most teams struggled to find a way to lift the items over the bearer, while some teams realized that a gap on the side of the arctic ice allowed them slip the items in behind the bearer that way—no lifting required.

So while some missions are straightforward, most have more than one solution. Be creative, but don't go crazy; simple designs and solutions are what win the event.

Grouping Missions into Zones

Once you have an understanding of the game missions and their rules, I have found it best to group the game layout into zones. The zones should be based on geographical location on the game table. Look at what missions are in the same relative area. Now, just because missions are close together doesn't mean that you should plan on doing them at the same time. The zoning is really more to help compartmentalize the game field and keep it from becoming overwhelming to your team.

You don't have to try to solve the missions at this point; just try to break the game field into two to four zones that are relative in location and give you a good idea where things are in relation to your robot. By creating these zones and understanding the rules, you will start to get a feel of what kinds of tasks your robot will be required to do. This is working up to the actual robot design. In Figure 1–1, you can see an example of the FLL 2009 Smart Move field broken into three workable zones.

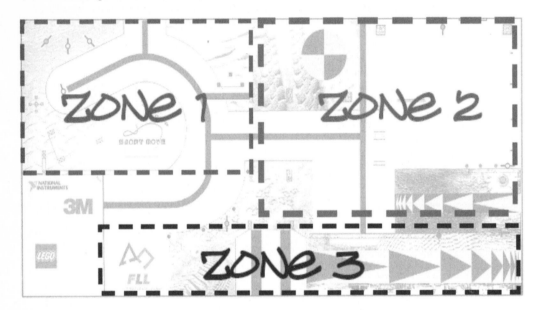

Figure 1–1. *The FLL Smart Move field broken into zones*

Tasking the Missions

You've studied the rules of the robot and the rules of the game and broken the game field into zones. But you're still not ready to build a robot; you're close but not there yet. Now that you know the rules, you must create your requirements by listing the tasks needed to complete the missions. Until you know the requirements for the missions, you still cannot design a robot to meet those requirements.

When tasking the missions, don't worry about getting every task exactly right, and of course, you can change the tasks as you try out what you. The goal is to get an idea of the actions the robot is going to need to do to complete the mission. This is a good time to get the entire team involved. Either break up the missions for different team members to task out, or do it as a large brainstorming session.

With each mission, you should write out the steps required in detail, such as, move forward three inches, turn right 90 degrees, and stop. Using a worksheet for each mission is a good idea. A mission worksheet should include a description of the mission, any rules required to complete the mission, the number of points the mission is worth, and maybe a priority and difficulty level. Figure 1–2 shows an example of a task list for a simple mission to collect some green loops.

Mission Name	Description	Task List
Collect Loops from North East Corner (30 points)	Must collect all three green loops from the North East Corner and return to base	- Move forward 6 inches - Turn 90 degrees north - Go forward to red wall - Turn right at red wall - Move forward 8 inches - Grab loops with claw - Close claw - Back up 5 inches - Turn 45 degrees south - Move forward to base

Figure 1–2. Sample task list

Spend some time carefully going over each mission and the tasks required to complete it. Once you have all the missions tasked out, sit down as a team and prioritize the missions. How you prioritize is completely up to you and your team. You may want to put them in order of highest points to lowest, or hardest to easiest.

If you don't want to make your own worksheets, you can find lots of them available online from various groups. Shortly after the FLL missions are announced, you will find various organizations that have already put together very helpful worksheets that you can start using right away.

I would suggest tackling some of the easier missions first when you actually start building and programming for the mission. By getting some of the easier missions out of the way, you will build confidence with your team and quickly be able to find any design flaws with your robot.

Mapping Out the Field

Now that you have your field broken into zones and your missions tasked out, it would be a good time to make a map of the game field. This document gives you a visual image of what path your robot will take on the game field for each mission.

Just like with the mission worksheets, you will find that many organizations will have created nice page-size maps of the current FLL game field. I recommend taking advantage of these resources; there's no need to duplicate effort if the resources are already available. Be sure to keep all of these maps organized along with your worksheets, so you can make updates as you modify or change missions.

When you have your maps done, you will start to see two things: first, if you have any missions that follow very similar paths, and second, if you have any obstacles that you would not be aware in the intended path of your robot. In Figure 1–3, you can see a sample map for the FLL 2008 Climate Connections field.

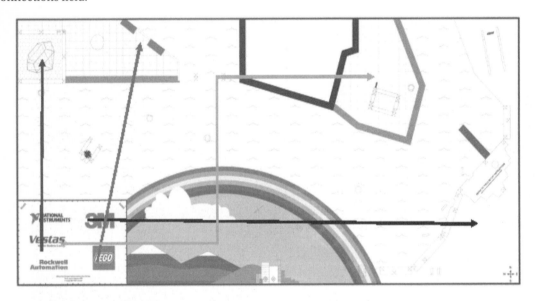

Figure 1–3. Sample mapping for FLL Climate Connections game field

Finding similar paths will help you as you progress in the design process and allow you to possibly combine missions and their tasks. You don't to combine missions when you first start, but as you fine-tune things, you will find that combining missions and sharing tasks will help you save time. We will talk about this later in the book as you begin to better organize your programs and tasks.

Obstacles are another concern that you may not be aware of until you start to think through the actual paths that your robot will take through your missions. Also, some obstacles may not be present until other missions have completed. For example, an object may get moved or pushed into your intended path during a pervious mission. This kind of finding could help you decide on the order of running your missions as well. Keep these obstacles in mind when thinking of the actual design of your robot.

Working with Constraints and Obstacles

By this point, you should be getting a very good feeling of what will be required of your robot to complete most of the missions. But we're not ready to build a robot just yet. There still other things to think about, things that may be in the way of your robot while it tries to perform the missions on the game field.

Field Obstacles

FLL 2008 Climate Connections, which had a very wide open field layout with few objects blocking the path of the robot to reach the missions, left a lot of room for large robots to move about without the fear of hitting anything. The following year's challenge, Smart Move, had a field full of various obstacles and quickly made teams realize that big and bulky wasn't going to be the winning design with this challenge. In Figure 1–4, you can see how crowded the field layout was for the 2009 Smart Move challenge.

Figure 1–4. Smart Move field layout

When dealing with obstacles on the field, read the rules carefully. With some items, moving the object out of your way may be a valid strategy, while other objects may be fixed in place and not allowed to be intentionally moved by your robot. Of course, your robot may not always be able to avoid certain items on a field. The referee will decide if you robot damages a fixed obstacle on purpose or by accident, so it's best to avoid running into these objects.

In FLL, the robot maximum size is basically an imaginary cube limited by the dimensions of the base on the game field and can be no more than 16 inches tall while in base; once the robot leaves base, it can expand to any size it needs. So when we talk about robot size, it's easiest to think of a cube that your robot would fit inside. Again, these size limitations only apply to a robot when it's starting in the base; once it starts moving under its own power, it is allowed to expand as much as necessary.

Environmental Obstacles

Besides obstacles included on the game field as part of the actual game, there will be various environmental obstacles. These are not necessarily intentional obstacles but are going to be there nonetheless, and many of them will be hard for your robot to prepare to handle.

The field mat surface in FLL is a plastic mat that spends a great deal of its life rolled up, thus giving a nice wavy, bumpy field at times. Your practice field will have laid out flat after a few days of being set up and should become fairly smooth, but the fields that you compete on at your actual event may not have the advantage of being set up ahead of time and given time to lay perfectly flat. Notice the bumps in the field mat shown in Figure 1–5; these types of obstacles can cause many team headaches and an unexpected surprise on the morning of competition. We will talk about ways to deal with this in Part 2 of this book, "Navigation."

Figure 1–5. *A bumpy game field mat*

Field tables can vary considerably at different competition events. Even though most events will publish a set of instructions on how to construct the game tables so that they remain uniform at each event location, this is not always the case. The best trick is to make sure your robot is not overly dependent on the surface or the edges of the field table construction. In later chapters, we will talk about how to take advantage of the table edges while avoiding any pitfalls of irregular table construction or materials.

Lighting is the one of the biggest things that will trip up a new team. You can practice for months in your classroom or basement and have your robot working flawlessly in the lighting of your room and then find that the lighting at the competition is completely different, causing various shadows or over exposures that you had not planned on with your robot. Also, if windows in the room allow natural light to shine on the game fields, the lighting conditions could actually change as the day progresses. Shielding your light sensors with your robot design and properly calibrating them can help you prevent lighting from ruining your day. In Chapter 5, we will talk about various ways to calibrate your light sensors.

Choosing Software

Before you team gets too far into the design process, you must decide what software you wish to use to program your robot. Many different options available for programming MINDSTORM NXT bricks, but only two are allowed to be used in FLL events: NXT-G and ROBOLAB. If you're building a robot for something other than FLL, be sure to carefully check the rules in regards to software choices.

Both NXT-G and ROBOLAB are visual programming languages created by LabVIEW for use with LEGO MINDSTORMS NXT bricks. NXT-G is shipped with your FLL robot kit and is included in the LEGO MINDSTORM retail kit as well. ROBOLAB must be purchased separately from LEGO Education. Both have their advantages and disadvantages. Here's a quick glance at a few of the differences:

- ROBOLAB supports events, while NXT-G does not.

- NXT-G supports using Bluetooth with the NXT brick; ROBOLAB does not.

Even though both are graphical programming languages, NXT-G condenses some functionality into more compact visual blocks. For examples Figures 1–6 and 1–7 show a simple program that drives a robot forward for 7 seconds.

Figure 1–6. NXT-G Move example

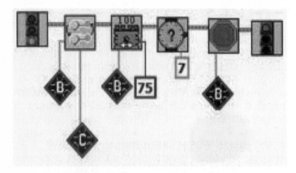

Figure 1–7. ROBOLAB Move example

You can see that the ROBOLAB example has a lot more visual icons involved. Some users will find ROBOLAB great because it gives them much flexibility at making low-level decisions for their robots, while others will tend to find it just a lot of extra work.

Table 1–1 shows a comparison of some of the features between the two software systems. This is not an all-inclusive list, but it will give you a nice look as some of the differences between the two systems.

Table 1–1. Compairison of NXT-G and ROBOLAB Features

Feature	NXT-G	ROBOLAB
Current version	2.0	2.9
Windows support	Yes	Yes
Mac OS X support	Yes	Yes
Bluetooth to PC	Yes	No
Events	No	Yes

Remember that you can only use one language or the other. Each language has its own firmware that must be loaded onto the NXT brick, and a single NXT kit cannot run both ROBOLAB and NXT-G programs on the same firmware. Another thing to consider is whether you plan on using a Mac or a Windows computer for programming your robot. This is important, because even though you can run NXT-G on both operating systems, the programs will not be interchangeable between the computers, so you will need to pick one platform and stick with it throughout your competition season.

Both software languages receive frequent code and firmware upgrades. Keeping your robot and computer up to date is very important, since some of these updates will actually be fixing bugs in the current release versions. How to perform these updates will be covered in Chapter 12 later in the book.

Introducing ROBOLAB

ROBOLAB software uses an icon-based, diagram-building environment to write programs that control the NXT brick. Many teams and schools that have been working with LEGO robots for a long time will have earlier copies of ROBOLAB from the days of using the older RCX LEGO MINDSTORM brick. One of the advantages of using ROBOLAB is that it will work with both the older RCX and NXT. Figure 1–8 shows an example of the ROBOLAB interface.

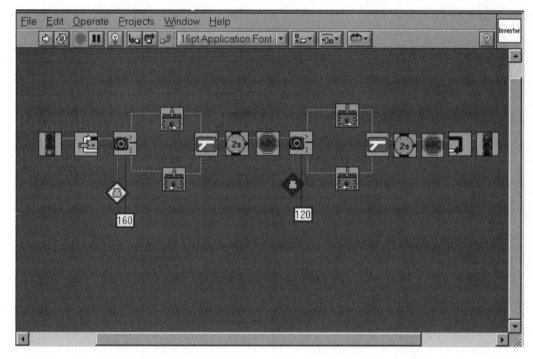

Figure 1–8. The ROBOLAB interface

ROBOLAB tends to require a bit more learning for students to pick up because of some of its more advance programming abilities. Depending on your robot strategies for handling the missions, these advance features may or may not be needed, so don't overcomplicate things just for the sake of doing so.

There are three programming approaches available with the ROBOLAB software:

- *Pilot* is a basic environment where programs are built using a click-and choose interface.

- *Inventor* provides a more open-ended, icon-based environment.

- *Investigator* uses Pilot and Inventor programming to incorporate data collection into projects.

With a normal FLL robot, you would typically use the Inventor mode when programming your robot to handle mission tasks.

If you or your team has never used ROBOLAB before, be sure to give yourselves plenty of time to work on learning the software before you get too far into your robot design and programming process. If your time is limited and you are new to ROBOLAB, I recommend sticking with NXT-G solely because of the time required to become efficient in ROBOLAB. You will find that most things you want to do with your robot do not require the more advanced features of ROBOLAB.

Introducing NXT-G

NXT-G is a visual programming language similar to ROBOLAB and was developed exclusively for the NXT brick by LabVIEW. Figure 1–9 shows an example of the NXT-G programming interface.

NXT-G 2.0 is the current version available from LEGO Education and shipped with the most recent LEGO MINDSTORM robotics kits. The feature set included with NXT-G is very straightforward and easy for a new team to learn. NXT-G has the advantage of being simpler and with fewer programming elements than ROBOLAB. Even with its simplicity, NXT-G can handle all that a robot needs to do to complete the task you have defined for your missions.

Even though NXT-G offers a wide variety of programming elements, many custom elements are available for download from various sources on the Internet. Be warned, though, that FLL rules do not allow the use of these elements; only the elements that were originally shipped with the NXT-G software are allowed. If you are building a robot for something other than FLL, be sure to check with the rules before using any third-party features for NXT-G.

■ **Note** This book will not go into great detail on how to use NXT-G; many great books and web sites are dedicated to NXT-G programming. James Floyd Kelly's book, *LEGO MINDSTORMS NXT-G Programming Guide*, *2ⁿᵈ Edition*, (Apress, 2010) is an excellent guide to NXT-G programming. Most of the software examples used in the following chapters will use NXT-G though.

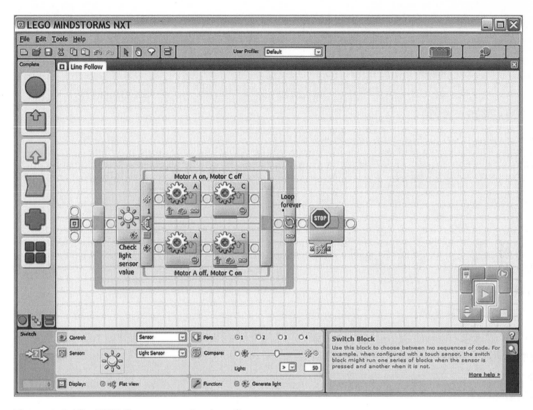

Figure 1–9. The NXT-G programming interface

Understanding the LEGO MINDSTORMS Hardware

One of the great things about LEGO robotics is the wide selection of pieces you have to choose from when you design your robot. In events such as FLL, any part made by LEGO is allowed to be used on your robot, with a few exceptions that we discussed earlier in this chapter. So be creative; spend some time just looking at the various LEGO pieces you have available to you either in the LEGO MINDSTORMS kit or your own collection of parts.

What I want to cover here are some of the electronic parts and sensors included with the LEGO MINDSTORMS kits so that you can better understand how they can be used in your robot design. It's important to understand how each part works so that you make the best use of it on your robot. Also, realize that using a part just for the sake of using it is not a good idea; keeping your robot simple is a big key to building a winning design.

NXT Intelligent Brick

The NXT brick is the brains of your robot—inside the NXT brick is a microcomputer. Figure 1–10 shows the standard NXT brick, which is an intelligent, computer-controlled LEGO brick that brings your robot to life. This is where all your sensors and motors will connect, where your programs will live, and where all the thinking will be done.

Figure 1–10. *NXT intelligent brick*

Like most computers, the NXT brick does only what you tell it to do. It will not make assumptions or guess at what you want it to do. Many times, I have heard students try to blame the robot for misbehaving or doing the wrong thing, but after a bit of research, they always find that the problems is with their program and that the NXT brick is doing exactly what they told it to do.

Even though the NXT brick is basically a toy, the computer processing power of this little computer is more powerful that the computers used on the Apollo 11 moon mission. Here is a quick break down of the NXT brick processor; you don't need to learn this level of detail, but it's interesting to know:

- 32-bit ARM7 microcontroller, with 256KB of flash memory and 64KB RAM

- 8-bit AVR microcontroller, with 4KB of flash memory and 512 bytes RAM

- Bluetooth wireless communication (Bluetooth Class II V2.0 compliant)

- Full-speed USB port (12 megabits per second)

- 4 input ports and a 6-wire cable digital platform (one port includes an IEC 61158 Type 4/EN 50 170 compliant expansion port for future use)

- 3 output ports and a 6-wire cable digital platform

- A 100×4–pixel LCD graphical display

- A loudspeaker with 8 kHz sound quality, as well as a sound channel with 8-bit resolution and a 2 to 16 kHz sample rate.

- Power source (6 AA batteries)

The NXT brick has four input ports for attaching sensors (ports 1, 2, 3, and 4) plus three output ports for attaching motors (ports A, B, and C). Also, on the front of the NXT brick, there are a series of buttons:

- *Orange button*: Use this for the commands On, Enter, and Run.

- *Grey arrows*: Use these to navigate options on the LCD display.

- *Dark grey button*: Use this for the commands Stop, Clear, and Back.

One important thing to bear in mind when designing your robot is to keep access to the NXT brick simple. You will need to be able to push the buttons on the NXT brick, so be sure not to block them or cover them up. This is also true for the sensor and motor ports. Also on the NXT brick, you will see a USB port used to connect your robot to your computer. Since Bluetooth communication is not allowed in FLL events, you will need to utilize the USB port for downloading your programs; keep access to this port unblocked as well.

Another consideration that will affect your design is what type of power your NXT brick will use. If you choose to use regular batteries, you will need to insure that you can remove the NXT brick quickly and easily without causing damage to your robot when changing batteries. If you use the rechargeable battery pack, make sure that your design does not block the port where the battery charger must be attached. It will be a good idea to keep the rechargeable battery LEDs visible as well; these LEDs indicate if the battery is charging or if the charge has completed.

Touch Sensor

The Touch Sensor (see Figure 1–11) allows your robot to have a sense of touch. The Touch Sensor tells the NXT brick when it has been pressed or released. This information will be very powerful in both navigation and object manipulation. The Touch Sensor can have various mounting points on your robot depending on the type of touching you wish to detect. Later in Parts 2 and 3, "Navigation" and "Manipulation," I will talk in detail about ways to take advantage of the Touch Sensor. In FLL, you are allowed to use only two Touch Sensors on your robot.

Figure 1–11. *An NXT Touch Sensor*

Light Sensor

The Light Sensor (see Figure 1–12) is one of the two sensors that will give your robot vision. The Light Sensor can read either ambient light levels or reflected light off of a surface. Like the Touch Sensor, the Light Sensor can be a major tool in helping your robot navigate the playing field. When including the Light Sensor on your robot design, keep in mind that if you are using it for reflective light detection, such as line following, you'll want to mount it in such a way that it is blocked from outside light sources. In later chapters, I will talk about how to best use the Light Sensor and how to calibrate it for various light sources. In FLL, your robot is allowed to have two Light Sensors.

Figure 1–12. An NXT Light Sensor

Ultrasonic Sensor

Like the Light Sensor, the Ultrasonic Sensor (see Figure 1–13) will also give the power of vision to your robot. Instead of detecting light, the Ultrasonic Sensor will send out sound waves to hit a surface and return. It will measure distance by calculating the time it takes for the sound wave to return after bouncing off the surface. Large flat surfaces are the easiest to detect with the Ultrasonic Sensor; round or thin objects are very difficult for the Ultrasonic sensor to detect. FLL allows robots to use only one Ultrasonic Sensor.

Figure 1–13. An NXT Ultrasonic Sensor

■ **Note** Two or more Ultrasonic Sensors can interfere with each other if they are within close proximity. When using these sensors in a robot design, this should be kept in mind.

Servo Motor

The Servo Motor (see Figure 1–14) not only gives your robot the ability to move but has a built-in Rotation Sensor. In older LEGO MINDSTORMS kits, a separate Rotation Sensor was required. The NXT brick has three motor ports allowing you to use two motors for navigation and other motor for manipulation. This is consistent with FLL rules, which allow for three motors to be used on your robot. The placement of your motors on the robot will depend on what type of drive system you decide on using. In Chapter 2, I will cover some of the various design styles that are commonly used.

Figure 1–14. *An NXT Servo Motor*

Beginning the Design Process

Now, you know the rules; you understand the mission task, and you are familiar with the major LEGO MINDSTORMS robot components. So how do you start putting together your robot design? This will be one of your first major challenges as a team. Getting a team to decide on single design can be quite a challenge all by itself, so this is a great opportunity for the team to work together in coming up with a solution.

Brainstorming as a Team

One way to get ideas flowing is to have the team gather together around a large pad of paper or, better yet, a white board and just start throwing out ideas. Either take turns drawing out ideas, or elect to have one person draw the ideas while others describe what they are thinking. This may seem like chaos, but it's a really good way to let everyone share their ideas and try to work down to one or two beginning designs.

Remember that these designs are far from being the final robot designs; they are just starting points. The robot design will evolve as you work through the mission tasks and tackle different design issues that arise as you test out your design. Every robot needs a start, and this brainstorming session is a good one. Figure 1–15 shows a white board after multiple design ideas have been noted. It may look like a mess, but talking about your ideas as a group helps everyone build on ideas and brings out concepts that no one may have thought of on their own.

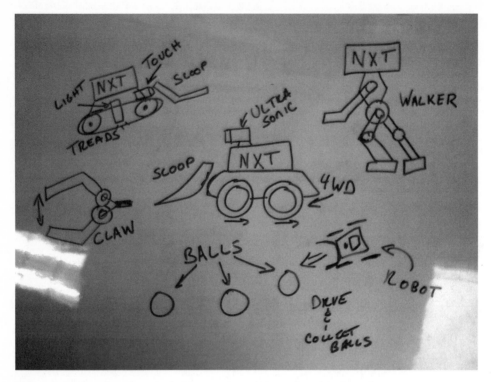

Figure 1–15. Results of a team brainstorming session on a white board

Be sure to encourage anyone's ideas during these sessions; there are no wrong answers or too-crazy ideas at this point of the process. Have fun with it; some of the best designs come from a crazy idea. It's also great for team members to build on each other's ideas.

Presenting Your Design

If your team desires a bit less free-form method for coming up with designs, you can have team members sit down alone or in pairs and come up with design ideas. Again, this doesn't have to be anything detailed or complicated at this point; just a simple sketch is good.

Once everyone has their ideas ready, they present them to the group. Each team member needs to not only show his or her diagrams but also explain why this design could be the winning design. When presenting the design to the team, be sure to include key points about the design that coincide with the mission task laid out earlier by the team. Also, be sure the design follows the event rules that you learned. Once all the design ideas have been presented, allow time for team members to discuss what they have seen and see if they can maybe blend some of the ideas together; its very unlikely that a single design is the perfect idea but more likely that a combination of the various designs will lead to a usable solution.

Drawing Your Design

No matter what process you used to come up with a starting design, you should draw a sketch of what you want the robot to look like. This sketch will not only help everyone on the team remember what you're planning on building but it's a good road map to use as you continue to improve your design. The drawing doesn't have to be overly detailed; just include the basic concepts. For example, in Figure 1–16, you can see the design includes large drive wheels, a caster rear wheel, and some kind of claw for grabbing loops.

Figure 1–16. Hand-drawning a robot brainstorming design

Keeping a sketch pad of all of your design idea is a great way to start your team documentation that will prove to be very helpful in the final organization process. I'll cover this more in the chapters in Chapter 13.

■ **Note** Save all your design diagrams, even the ones you don't use. All of these are great reminders of how you got to the final design and can be helpful when you have to explain your design process to robot technical judges at your completion.

Resource Contention

Before you build your robot as a team, there is one more thing to consider—contention. Building robots as a team introduces a dynamic that does exist when one person builds a LEGO robot. *Contention* occurs when multiple people need to access a single resource. That resource could be the computer for programming or the robot itself. Contention can cause frustration among team members as they vie for use of this single resource.

One way to solve a contention problem is to have multiple resources. For example, a class or team might have multiple copies of the robot. This works in theory, but most classes lack the resources to give everyone a robot. Instead, most teams divide into groups of two or three students.

If you do not have the advantage of having multiple robot kits and the team must share a single robot, it might be best to set up a schedule of some kind where team members working on a particular task schedule the robot for a certain time period. This will allow everyone to schedule their time better and not spend a lot of time sitting around not knowing when they can use the robot. It will be a good idea to lay down some rules as well in regards to changes made to the robot; you don't want someone making major changes to the robot design without consulting the rest of the team, since this could have a big effect on mission designs other team members have already developed.

In FLL, most teams work with a single robot. One robot always seems to run the programs best, and a program for a particular robot design always seems to run slightly differently on the backup robot than it does on the main robot. Also, even though NXT bricks are manufactured the same way, variations between identically built robots always seems to occur. It may be that the motors on one robot are newer or that the LEGO parts on the other hold together slightly differently. In precision LEGO robotics, little things matter a lot!

Summary

You can see that there is a lot more to designing a winning robot besides snapping a bunch of LEGO bricks together. If you take the time to understand the rules and map out your plan of attack, you will find that you will be in a much stronger position when you actually get to building your robot. As with everything, planning ahead will save you hours of backing up and doing things over.

No matter what design your team decides on building, the true key to a winning robot is still going to be practice, practice, and more practice. It doesn't matter how awesome your robot is if you don't know how to make it work effectively and consistently.

CHAPTER 2

■ ■ ■

Chassis Design

You're ready to build your robot, but what kind of robot design do you need? You know the rules and the requirements, so now you need a design will best meet your goal of a winning robot. No single design will ensure a winner. The goal is a robot that can deliver consistent results over and over again. And it must be able to perform with the same consistently in different environments. The first part of meeting that goal is to start with a sturdy and effective chassis.

I have found one of the better ways to build a chassis is to start with the drive system and work my way up, this allows room to experiment and see what work design best works. Don't forget to make room for the motors to attach, but you can get a lot done before the first motor is put in place.

Here, we'll cover some design aspects and LEGO elements that can be used in your chassis design. Understanding the principles is important but so is experimenting. Play with the parts in your kit and see how they fit together and interact with each other. You may come up with some variations that someone has never tried before.

Understanding Basic Design Aspects

Designing your winning robot is going to require balancing size, power, and speed. These three principles are connected with each other; for example, the faster your robot can travel, the less power it will possess. The bigger your robot, the slower it will become, because it will require more power to move. The more power your robot has, the slower it will travel.

You will need to think of your requirements and decide what things are important for your robot. Does it need to be fast? Will it have to push a lot of things and thus need to be strong? Are there lots of small places on the game field that your robot will need to access, thus requiring a small robot? These are the kinds of questions you will need to keep in mind when while you learn about chassis designs.

Size

When building your robot, try to decide how big you want it, but don't think so much about exact size; think more generally. Imagine the desired size as a box; the goal is to keep your robot small enough to fit within that box. With LEGO robots, it is very easy to get carried away with their size. Adding new parts is easy, so things can quickly get out of control.

Remember, even though LEGO parts are relatively lightweight, their weight will add up quickly, and soon, you'll find that you have built something that is going to require a lot of motor power to move around the game field.

Power

When I speak of power, I'm talking about the strength of your robot. Some robots need to push heavy things or even pull some objects. If this is the case, your robot is going to be required to be very strong. Even though we're dealing with LEGO robots, if you gear one correctly, they can produce a great deal of torque, thus giving your robot a lot of power. You do need to be careful, because if you overdo the power, you will break some pieces. I've seen many LEGO gears and axles twisted and snapped from being having too much torque applied.

Speed

No one wants a slow robot; we all love build things that go fast. In FLL, you only have 2.5 minutes to complete as many missions as you can, so speed is important. But remember: in gaining speed, the effectiveness of other design principles, such as power and size, will be sacrificed. It's not easy for a big robot to go fast. Also with speed, the risk of mistakes can increase; it's easy for a speedy robot to miss goals. Many times, it's hard for a fast robot to be accurate, so it's a good idea to start out slowly and then increase the speed as you practice your missions.

Batteries

Even though I didn't list batteries as one of the design aspects, they do have an effect on all three of the principles—size, power, and speed. Obviously, the faster your robot runs, the more battery power it will consume. The same goes with motor power; producing more torque means consuming more battery power as well. These are things you need to keep in mind with your robot design. With LEGO MINDSTORMS robots, you only have a few battery choices, and only two have an effect on the actual size of your robot design.

You can use replaceable or rechargeable AA batteries. If you choose to do this, you will be replacing batteries quite often during practices and competitions. Keep this in mind for your chassis design, and give yourself easy access to the batteries.

Even though the FLL game is only 2.5 minutes long, you will want fresh batteries for each run to ensure consistent performances from your robot. Also, be sure to always use the same type of batteries, running on Alkaline batteries at the beginning of a season and then switching to Lithium batteries will cause big differences in your robot's performance, most likely unexpected and undesired behaviors. So be consistent with your battery choice.

The easiest thing to do for batteries is to use the LEGO MINDSTORMS rechargeable battery pack. This is included with the FLL robot kit and can be purchased separately from LEGO Education as well. Even though the rechargeable battery packed actually runs at a slightly lower voltage than AA batteries, it will produce a more consistent power level for a longer period of time. Remember, consistency is a good thing for LEGO robots.

Be sure to keep the size and location of the recharger port on the battery pack in mind when building your robot. The battery pack will add about a quarter inch to the thickness of your NXT brick, and this could affect the design if you were originally using the changeable AA batteries. The recharger port needs to located in such a way that you can plug in the charger with out having to remove the battery or the NXT from the robot. You'll also want to be able to see the charger indicator lights on the battery pack so that you know you're connected and getting a good charge. Nothing is worse than leaving the robot charging to only find out later that that plug wasn't connected properly and it didn't charge at all.

Finding the Center of Gravity

For your robot to perform consistently, it will need to be properly balanced; all wheels or threads need to keep in contact with the game field at all times to ensure consistency and repeatability during each mission run. A robot that tips over or wobbles will be very hard to control and program for dependable mission attempts. Balance depends on a couple of things: the center of gravity and the wheelbase of the robot. The wheelbase is any area within a region created by drawing lines between each of the wheels on your robot, as shown in Figure 2–1. The area with in this region is the wheelbase of your robot. For your robot to stay balanced, the center of gravity should be inside the wheelbase; the closer to the center of the wheelbase that the center of gravity is located, the more balanced the robot will become.

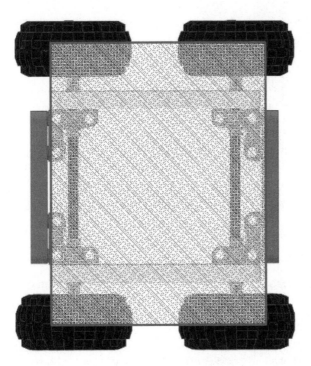

Figure 2–1. The wheel base of a four-wheel robot chassis

For a robot to stay balanced and stable, the center of gravity needs to stay within the wheel base area of the robot; otherwise, the robot could lose its balance and tip over.

The center of gravity is the point of the average location of the weight for the robot. This is not the center of your robot, but the point at which the weight is equal above and below and on all sides. There are multiple ways to find the center of gravity of your robot design; the easiest is to simply balance your robot on a fulcrum of some kind. Balancing the robot front to back will find your longitudinal balance plane (see Figure 2–2), and balancing it from side to side will find your lateral balance plane (see Figure 2–3).

Figure 2–2. Balancing the robot to find the longitudinal balance plane

Figure 2–3. Balancing the robot to find the lateral balance plane

The intersection of these two planes will be the line along which your robot's center of gravity is located. You will need to find the vertical balance plane to pinpoint the center of gravity.

To find the vertical balance plane, tilt your robot up on either its front or back and gently try to balance the robot without letting it fall. Once you feel the robot is balanced, line up a ruler with the vertical plane. The place where this plane intersects the longitudinal and the lateral planes will be your center of gravity.

Keep in mind that you need to build your robot in such a way that all your wheels are touching the ground and have equal weight resting on them. When you start adding attachments to your robot, they could change the center of gravity considerably and put your robot off balance again. We will talk more about that in Chapters 8 and 9, but do keep in mind that you may need to add some kind of counterweight or shift your center of gravity to make room for attachments.

Another concern that can affect your robot's balance is inertia. Ever been riding your bike and then slammed on the brakes really hard? How did your body react when the bike stopped? It most likely kept moving forward, in some cases your body, or even the bike, may have been lifted up. When you felt this happening you experienced Newton's first law of motion. This behavior of objects is called *inertia*, and it effects your robot's balance as well. The formula to calculate inertia is simple; its force equals mass times acceleration ($F = ma$).

■ **Note** Newton's first law of motion says that an object in motion will stay in motion and an object at rest will stay at rest unless acted on by an unbalanced force.

A robot with a high center of gravity can become unbalanced if it's moving and then stops, turns a corner, or climbs an incline. All of these scenarios can be avoided by locating the center of gravity low on the robot and in the center of the wheelbase. Robots with wide wheelbases are going to handle the effects of inertia much better than robots with small wheelbases.

Gearing Up

Your robot is going to need to move, and how fast or powerfully you want it to move may determine how you set the gears on it. The current NXT motors have some built-in gear ratios that make them acceptable for direct drive to your wheels if desired. But if you want something a bit faster, or better yet stronger, adding some drive gears could be the way to go. Gears can also be used to change the direction or axis of the rotation or even to change rotation to a linear movement.

The LEGO MINDSTORMS kit offers an array of different gear types:

- Spur
- Crown
- Bevel
- Double bevel
- Worm
- Pulleys
- Knob

The following subsections describe each of these types. You'll learn how each type works and what it is best used for.

Spur Gears

Spur, or straight-cut, gears (see Figure 2–4) are the simplest of gears; they are what most people envision when you talk about gears. When you are simply trying to transfer power from one location to another along a straight line, these are the types of gears that you would most likely use. The teeth are straight and aligned parallel to the axis of motion. To work correctly spur gears must be combined with other gears on parallel axles.

Figure 2–4. *24-tooth spur gears inline together*

Crown Gears

Crown gears (see Figure 2–5) have teeth that are raised on the edges, giving them a crown-like appearance. They are normally used when axles are meeting at a right angle, but they can also be used in the same manner as a spur gear if needed.

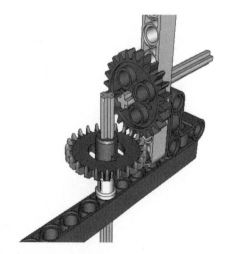

Figure 2–5. *A crown gear meeting a spur gear at a 90-degree angle*

Bevel Gears

There are two types of bevel gears: straight-tooth and spiral-tooth. LEGO only makes straight-tooth bevel gears (see Figure 2–6). Bevel gears have a slightly conical shape and are useful when axles meet at a right angle in a small space. The bevel gears are much smaller than crown gears and work well in tight situations; they also cause less friction that a crown gear. Angles other than 90 degrees are possible, but using bevel gears at those angles runs the risk of slippage. Also bevel gears, unlike crown gears, can only be used with other bevel gears.

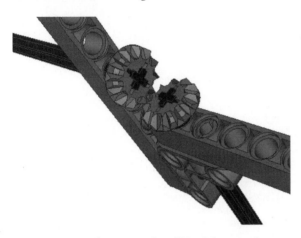

Figure 2–6. Bevel gears work well in tight areas but can only be paried up with other bevel gears.

Double Bevel Gears

The double bevel gear (see Figure 2–7) is a great mixture between the spur gear and the bevel gear. The double bevel comes in various sizes and allows for a smooth meshing of teeth at various angles. It can be used in parallel and in various angles, and the double bevel can be used with various other gears as well.

In today's NXT robots, double bevel gears are the most popular. Not only are the gears versatile but they tend to mesh together better than the traditional spur gears, giving a smoother motion to your robot and less friction between the gears.

Figure 2–7. Pair of Double Bevel gears meshing at 90 degrees.

Worm Gears

Worm gears are similar to a screw (see Figure 2–8); they have threading that runs along the outside of a cylinder. When meshed with a spur gear at a right angle, the worm gear can create a very high gear ratio. The worm gear will move one rotation for each tooth on the connected spur gear; this is an n:1 (n-to-1) reduction. A worm gear meshed with a 24-tooth gear will produce a 24:1 reduction. Nothing can beat the shear strength and size of a worm/spur gear combination for power, but be careful because the torque can be too much for some LEGO pieces and cause separation or actually break a piece.

It's important to note that the worm gear must be used as the input axle, since the output axle connected to a worm gear cannot turn the input axle. Basically, a worm gear can turn another gear, but another gear cannot turn a worm gear. This one-way relationship can work to your advantage for locking and holding things in place; it might not be so useful in chassis movement but is great for attachments.

Figure 2–8. A worm gear meshed with a 24-tooth spur gear in a technic gear box

Clutch Gears

Clutch gears (see Figure 2–9) are special because they are designed to allow the axle to rotate around the gear when the maximum allowable torque is applied to the gear. They contain an internal clutch that will slip and no longer move with the axle once the maximum force is applied. The LEGO 24-tooth clutch gear has "2.5-5 N.cm" printed on the front of it; this is the torque rating for the gear. The clutch gears are useful for saving motors and keeping your robot from breaking or tearing up itself when too much torque is applied to the gear. At this time, LEGO only produces one size of clutch gear.

Figure 2–9. *A clutch gear meshed with a 24-tooth spur gear*

Pulleys

Pulleys (see Figure 2–10) are unlike gears in that they do not have teeth but have grooves that hold belts in place. LEGO offers a variety of pulley and belt sizes. The ratio of the pulley sizes is similar to the ratios that we get when meshing gears together. Pulleys can be a great choice when trying to deliver power in unusual spaces that gears don't necessarily fit. The drawback of using pulleys is that they will slip when high amount of torque is applied to them, but this behavior can be used to your advantage as an alternative to the clutch gear for creating limited slip mechanisms. Just be careful of relying on pulleys too much in an FLL robot; the belts are not the most dependable for staying in place. You'd hate to have one shoot off during an event.

Figure 2–10. Pully wheels set up with red band

Knob Wheel

The knob wheel is an unusual type of gear; it doesn't even look like a gear (see Figure 2–11). But if you look at it closely, you'll realize that it is just a simple four-tooth gear. Similar to the bevel gear, the knob wheel is good for 90-degree, low-speed connections and for applying high torque in angles without the risk of gear slippage.

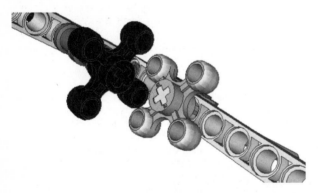

Figure 2–11. Two knob wheels meshed at 90 degrees

Gear Ratios

Knowing all the different gears is great, but how do you connect them together? It's important to understand gear ratios. The gear ratio is how much the output axle turns based on the rotation of the input axle. For example, if you have an eight-tooth gear on your input axle and a 24-tooth gear on your output axle, for every complete rotation of the input axle, the output axle would have turned one-third of the distance. This would produce a 3:1 gear reduction ratio, as in Figure 2–12.

Figure 2–12. An eight-tooth input gear meshed with two- tooth output gear for a 3:1 gear reduction

You can read this 3:1 ratio as saying that for every three turns of the input, the output will make one turn. When slowing down the rotation with gears, we call this *gearing down* or *gear reduction*, and it can increase the torque generated by the input source, such as a motor.

You can reduce the gears more by meshing gears of even higher differences in teeth count, such as combining an eight-tooth gear with a 40-tooth gear to produce a 5:1 reduction. For even greater reductions, you can join pairs of gears together. Two sets of 3:1 gears would produce a 9:1 reduction, as shown in Figure 2–13. You can continue this concept to create extensive gear reduction to produce far more torque than you'd ever need for an FLL robot.

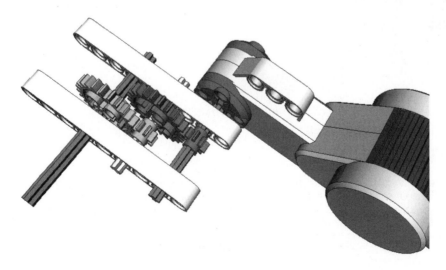

Figure 2–13. A pair of 3:1 gears joined together to produce a 9:1 gear reduction

As you can imagine, if you switched the input to the 24-tooth gear and the output to the eight-tooth gear, you would cause the gear ratio to switch as well. The new ratio would be 1:3; for every turn of the input axle, the output axle would turn three times. This is called *gearing up* and is a way to gain more speed from an input source, such as a motor.

When putting gears together, also note that an even number of gears will reverse the direction of the input, while an odd number of gears will keep the input traveling in the same direction, as shown in Figures 2–14 and 2–15.

Figure 2–14. *Two spur gears meshed together will reverse the rotation direction.*

Figure 2–15. *Three spur gears meshed together will maintain the current rotation direction.*

Getting Your Wheels

One of the most import decisions you will make in regard to your robot design choosing your wheels. Wheels are required to keep your robot stable, to help it handle various terrains, to make it go fast, and to keep it accurate during navigation. With the LEGO MINDSTORMS FLL kit, there are a variety of different tire and wheels to choose from; with the wide variety of wheels available from LEGO, it's hard to know which ones to choose. The larger the diameter of the tire, the faster your robot will travel, but as we talked about previously, a fast robot is not going to be as strong as a robot with smaller tires. So with your design considerations in mind, you will need to carefully think through your needs.

Circumference

Knowing the circumference of a tire is important when considering which wheels and tires you want on your robot. The circumference will be the distance that your robot will travel after the wheel has made one rotation, or more simply, it's the distance around the circle of your wheel (see Figure 2–16). Knowing this information will be very important when we talk more about navigation in future chapters.

For now, all you have to know is that to calculate the circumference, you simply multiply the diameter of your tire by pi (roughly 3.14), so C = πd. To determine the diameter of your wheel, simply lay the wheel on a ruler and measure the distance across the wheel at the widest outside part.

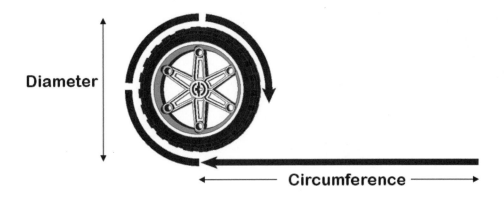

Figure 2–16. The circumference of a wheel

Mounting

When mounting wheels to your chassis, it's important to give your axles proper support. If your wheel is mounted close to the chassis, be sure to include a bushing so that the wheel does not get pressed against the chassis. At the same time, you do not want the wheel to be too far from the chassis unless it's supported correctly.

Most robot chassis use a cantilevered assembly to attach the wheels to the chassis. In Figure 2–17, you can see that a single bushing holds the wheel just the right distance to prevent it from rubbing the chassis and is only supporting the axle on one side. This creates friction on the axle as it is being pressed against the chassis. In Figure 2–18, the wheel has been placed further from the chassis with multiple bushings. Because the wheel is further away from the chassis more force is put on the axle and chassis, causing more friction between the two. Also, this setup is going to cause the wheel to camber and give us unpredictable results when trying to navigate. And over time, the axle itself will begin to bend, thus making the robot's performance even more unpredictable.

Figure 2–17. *Single bushing spacing on wheel axle*

Figure 2–18. *Multiple bushing spacing on a wheel axle, moving the wheel further from the chassis causing more friction*

The most dependable solution is to have a chassis that fully supports the wheel axle on both ends, giving maximum support the wheel and axle and removing a great deal of friction on the it; see Figure 2–19. We will cover this concept in more details in Chapter 3, and I'll explain the physics behind it. For now, you need to keep in mind that proper support of the axle and wheel are important your chassis design to ensure the reliability of your robot.

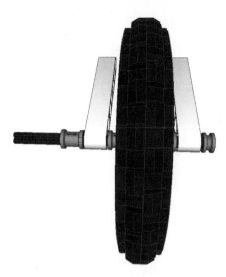

Figure 2–19. A wheel axle being supported on both ends, reducing friction on the axle

Treads

When a lot of people think of robots, they don't think of wheeled bots but of ones with treads, like many of the popular movie robots. One pair of treads comes in the LEGO MINDSTORMS kit.

Robots with treads tend to be very low to the ground and have a stable center of gravity; they can also be very agile in small places. Crossing bumpy and uneven ground is easy for them as well.

Even through treads are cool looking and very easy to build, they are not always the best choice for FLL robots. Unfortunately, treads are inaccurate when it comes to navigation. Precision turning is difficult, and even a simple task such as going straight suffers when driving on a flat surface. Treads tend to hop when driving, making accurate navigation on an FLL mat an extra challenge.

Exploring the Most Common Chassis

There are basically three types of robot chassis: those with wheels, those with treads, and those that walk. Chassis with wheels and treads are the most common in FLL. I've never seen a walker robot compete in FLL; although I'm not saying it can't be done, I'll stick with talking about common wheeled and tread designs.

Also *differential steering* (or *skid steer*) is the most common steering design in FLL robots. This is where two motors turning in opposite directions are used to steer the robot. In Chapter, 4 we will talk about steering techniques in greater detail.

Two-Wheeled Robots

One of the simplest designs is the two-wheeled robot design shown in Figure 2–20. This consists of two wheels, each attached to its own motor, with some kind of skids or ball casters to help the robot keep its balance. Depending on the game field, these designs can actually do very well in FLL events. Many times, the simple designs perform the best.

The center of gravity can be a concern with two-wheeled robots just because the wheels tend to be close to the front, and once any attachments are connected, this can cause the robots to fall forward. So it's always a good idea to test and retest the design as you add new features to your robot chassis to ensure that you have not shifted the center of gravity off-center in the wheelbase.

Figure 2–20. A two-wheeled robot with skids in the rear for balance

Three-Wheeled Robots

A very common LEGO robot design is the three-wheeled robot, or *tribot* (see Figure 2–21). The three-wheeled robot is similar to the two-wheeled robot but has a caster wheel instead of skids; the robot will have two wheels, each driven by a separate motor, and a caster wheel in the rear. The passive caster wheel will turn and travel in the direction of the robot. The third wheel is just in place to give balance to the robot chassis and to reduce friction on the game surface caused by skids.

Figure 2–21. *A three-wheeled robot with a caster wheel on rear*

Four-Wheeled Robots

Four-wheeled robots are much more stable that a two- or three-wheeled ones. Having a wheel on all four corners of the chassis provides a large area for the center of gravity, thus making the robot very stable and able to avoid losing its balance. Using differential steering on four-wheel robots is a bit more difficult than with two- or three-wheeled robots, but with proper programming, that issue can be overcome. In Chapter 4, we will talk about this more.

There are two types of four-wheeled robots: two-wheel drive and four-wheel drive.

Two-wheel drive works very similar to other robot designs in the fact that two of the wheels are each driven by single motors; the other two wheels are passive and just tagging along for the ride to add stability for the robot. Steering can be a challenge with two-wheel drive, since one wheel on each side of the robot is going to be skidding while the robot turns. If these wheels have good traction on the mat, they can cause a lot of resistance during the turn. Since these passive wheels are not being powered, they really don't need to have a tire (see Figure 2–22); you can run the wheels without tires to allow them to skid freely on the mat when turning.

A four-wheel drive robot is a bit more work to build; each pair of wheels on the side of the robot needs to be driven by a single motor. In most cases, this is going to require some type of gearing setup. Four-wheel drive is useful when you need to have a strong robot or one that can climb steep inclines. A four-wheel drive robot will steer the same way other differential steering robots do, but instead of having just two turning, two wheels will turn in one direction and two in the other. There will be some skidding by the wheels, but turning all will minimize this. Also, the closer the wheels are to each other, the less resistance they will encounter when turning.

Figure 2–22. A four-wheeled robot with two-wheel drive

Six-Wheeled Robots

Six-wheeled robot chassis are great when designed correctly. The wheel selection in the LEGO MINDSTORMS FLL kit is a bit limiting for such designs, but if you have access to some of the huge variety of other LEGO wheels, a six-wheeled robot can be done quite nicely. There are really two types of basic design ideas for a six-wheeled robot.

The first design option is very similar to the four-wheeled robot but with an extra set of wheels either in all-wheel-drive mode or still just two-wheel drive. If you need power, six-wheel drive works well but is not always the best choice for FLL challenges. Steering can become a bit challenge as well as navigating tight spaces. So even though using six wheels makes for a cool design, this is often not the best choice.

Now, the other six-wheeled design involves middle wheels that are larger or set lower that the wheels on the ends; this is sometimes referred to as a *West Coast chassis*. The idea is that the center wheels are the drive wheels, so when the robot turns, the balance of the robot will shift as needed to either the front or the rear wheels. However, the amount of friction during the turn is limited, since the balance will fall mainly on the center wheels.

For this design to work properly, your robot chassis needs to be balanced over the two middle drive wheels. When you do this properly, you can have a very nimble robot chassis that can still be of a substantial size, as shown in Figure 2–23.

Figure 2–23. *A six-wheeled robot*

Tracked Robots

A tracked robot can have a similar wheelbase to a wheeled robot, but of course, it's using a set of LEGO rubber tracks. The tracks give the robot chassis a very stable stance and a naturally low center of gravity (see Figure 2–24).

A tracked robot chassis is very helpful when tackling obstacles that involve crossing over an opening or uneven surfaces. The 2009 Smart Moves challenge featured a dyno-meter that the robots could cross to access part of the field; the spinning nature of the dyno-meter caused many of the wheeled robots great headaches, while the tracked robots tended to do better at making the crossing.

Unfortunately, the drawbacks in using tracks tend to outweigh the advantages. Tracked robot chassis have a hard time traveling in a straight line and tend to hop on a smooth surface. Also, keeping tension on the tracks can prove to be challenging at times. Often, a third wheel inside the tracks will help relieve any issues with tension but will not help the tracks to remain predictable during missions.

I don't want to discourage a team from using tracks on its robot, so try them if you like the idea of using them and they meet the requirements of your mission task. As with everything, experiment and see what works best for your situation.

Figure 2–24. A tracked robot

Troubleshooting

Once you have completed your chassis, if you find that it seems to be misbehaving and not moving smoothly, there are a few areas you should check. First, make sure all your gears are positioned at the correct distances and not meshing too hard or binding. Sometimes, gears seem to fit together but are causing too much friction because they're meshing too tightly with the other gears. Also, check all your bushings to ensure that none of them are pressing against the chassis too tightly. Wheel rub is another thing to check; if you don't put the correct spacers on the backs of your wheels, the wheels tend to slide some during practice and could rub your chassis and cause friction.

These are LEGO robots, and parts will move around even when you don't want them to. So it's a good idea to give your robot a good looking over before each event to see if anything has come loose or tighten up.

Summary

With any building project, having a good foundation is important to success. This is the same for a winning robot design. Before the robot can be expected to perform well, it needs to start out with a good chassis design. Many teams team to rush the design of the robot so that they can begin working on game missions and then later pay the price of having issues and frustrations because of a poor chassis design. Take the time to get the chassis design right.

PART 2

Navigation

■ ■ ■

CHAPTER 3

Going Straight

Once you've built your robot, you're going to want it to go somewhere, and everyone knows the shortest distance between two places is a straight line. In the world of LEGO robots, going straight is one of those things that is easier said than done. Many new teams in FLL will rely on *odometry*, or *dead reckoning*, to get their robot to the desired location on the game field. Odometry is when you use measurements as a way to navigate your robot a point on the field. You're simply telling the robot to go a predefined distance and using the rotation sensors built into your robots NXT servo to determine if you've gone the desired distance. The position will be estimated relative to your starting point. As you will find out, using odometry does not always land your robot where you expected.

Solely relying on odometry for navigation of your robot is not a good idea; a smart robot will find ways to incorporate navigation points on the game field and be able to analyze were it is in reference to its target using various methods and sensors. So odometry is really only a small part of robot navigation and should be used sparingly. In the FLL Smart Moves challenge, some field items were put in place to purposely limit the use of pure odometry in navigating the missions, so while it can be quick a way to get started on some missions, try not to rely on it too much.

In this chapter, we will talk about factors that will influence your robot's ability to go in a straight line and what you can do to improve its accuracy when trying to get to a desired position on the game field.

Design Influences

Besides the actual environment where your robot is performing, the physical design of your robot is going to have the biggest influence on how well it does at navigating a straight line. The main influences here are the wheelbase and a balanced robot chassis. This is where setting the center of gravity correctly will come into play.

Wheelbase

The wheelbase of your robot needs to be nice and wide; again, this is about keeping balance. If your robot is using four or more wheels, make sure all of them are actually touching the ground. Even though the design is created symmetrically, it is possible to build a four-wheel robot in which one wheel is not touching the ground, thus throwing off your robot's balance and causing it to wobble. A wobbly robot will not go straight consistently.

A wide, stable base is going to be a big factor in going straight. Think of trying to run forward with your feet close together; running becomes much easier when you move your feet apart and get a more stable stance. The same is true for a robot: a robot with a narrow wheelbase will quickly get off track with the slightest bump or imperfection in the game field surface, especially if this robot has an attachment that is moving or carrying cargo.

Also, the width of the actual wheels will have an effect. When going straight, a wider wheel with more rubber touching the field will travel much straighter than a skinny wheel with little contact to the field. However, the opposite is true for turning, so the trick is to find a happy medium between the two. For example, a four-wheel robot with rubber tires on all four wheels will track in a very straight line with little effort, but this very same robot will have a rough time when it comes to making a smooth turn.

So keep the center of gravity low and the stance balanced, and maintain just enough friction with the game field to travel evenly but not so much as to make turning an issue. If the wheels and chassis have too much friction with the field, getting the robot to turn smoothly can become an issue because most LEGO robots will be using some form of skid steering, meaning some part of the robot drags as the robot turns. So keeping the friction to a minimum will allow the turning movement to remain smooth and even.

Weight

Also related to balance is the weight of the robot. A heavy robot is normally more accurate, since the NXT servos are limited from spinning the wheels when the robot starts moving. Imagine if you're telling your robot to move forward four rotations, but when it starts moving, it spins the wheels the first quarter of the rotation. This, of course, is going to put your robot in a different ending position than you were expecting. So limit wheel slippage as much as possible, which you can do by not moving forward too quickly and by having a robot with some weight that will keep traction on the drive wheels.

A very lightweight robot is going to lose traction quickly, making it very hard to predict where it's going to end up when using odometry for navigation. Try to keep the majority of the weight over the drive wheels while still keeping the robot balanced. But don't go crazy and make your robot a total lead brick that's going to require all your power just to move forward. Most robot events, such as FLL, are under time limits, so your robot needs to be nimble enough to get the task done in the allotted timeframe.

Wheel Circumference

Knowing the circumference of your drive wheels is important when determining how far your robot is going to travel. If you program your Move block to turn four rotations, how far is your robot actually going to travel? This is where knowing your wheel's circumference is important; the circumference the distance the wheel will travel after one complete rotation as shown in Figure 3–1. As you learned in Chapter 2, the circumference equals pi times the diameter, so now, we get to use some math.

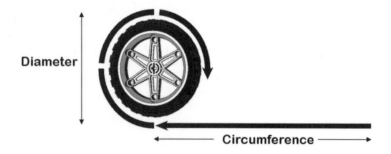

Figure 3–1. The circumference of a wheel

If our wheel has a circumference of 3 inches and we're moving four rotations, the expected result is that our robot will move forward 12 inches, the circumference times the number of rotations. If you need to calculate the necessary rotation for a 12-inch move, the formula would be rotation equals distance divided by circumference (or 4 = 12/3). This may seem very straightforward to understand, but many teams skip right over doing such calculations and just use trial and error to get the values for their rotations. And then, something changes with their robot, such as gear ratios or wheel size, and all their movements are miscalculated and they have to start over with the guessing process of determining the proper rotations.

However, if a team can understand the math behind calculating the proper rotations from the beginning, changes will have a very minimal effect on the team's current progress and will not prevent moving forward. Also, these calculations are good talking points the team should share with an event's robot design judges. Judges are much more impressed with teams that understand why their robots are performing the way that they are and can explain that to the judge. If a judge asked team members why they choose to use four rotations in their program and they simply state that they just kept trying numbers until something worked, it doesn't sound nearly as impressive as being able to explain the true mathematical reason why four is the correct number of rotations needed for the robot.

Don't forget to take any gear ratios into account when calculating the proper rotation. If you are not driving your wheel directly from the NXT servo but have some gearing in place, that will change the equation some. In that case, the rotation will be calculated as rotation equals distance divided by the circumference times the ratio. So for example, if you have a wheel with a circumference of 3 inches that is being driven by a servo hooked to a gear setup with a 3:1 ratio, your formula would be rotation = 12 / $(3 \times 1/3)$, giving you a rotation of 12 to travel 12 inches, one inch per rotation. What if the gear ratio is flipped to a 1:3 ratio?

Wheel Support

Proper wheel support and the reduction of friction on the wheel's axles are important to helping a robot track straight. If one drive wheel is receiving more or less friction that the other, the robot's ability to drive straight is going to be greatly diminished.

The typical robot is going to weigh between one and two pounds, which might not seem like a lot. However, your robot's motors are going to have to carry this weight all around the game field, so we need to make the job as easy as possible for the motors. The biggest issue for your robot's motors to overcome is friction.

In Chapter 2, which covered robot design, we talked about ways to mount your wheels to the robot, the most common being a cantilever. In this case, the wheel is mounted to one side of the axle with the axle being supported by a LEGO beam and then a bushing is added on the back of the wheel to prevent the axle and wheel from falling off the robot chassis. When being supported in this manner, the axle acts as a level and applies pressure to the LEGO beam, thus creating friction on the axle as it turns. The LEGO beam where the axle is supported becomes the fulcrum for the lever, so placement of the wheel on the axle will affect the force applied against the LEGO beam. For example, if the wheel is located far away from the LEGO beam on the axle, this will increase the amount of force being generated by the level, thus increasing the amount of friction on the movement of the axle, as shown in Figure 3–2.

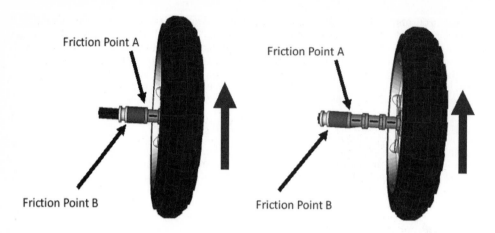

Figure 3–2. The further away the wheel is from the chassis, the more friction is being created at friction point A. Moving the wheel closer to the chassis will reduce the friction on the wheel's axle.

We can free up the axle by keeping the wheels close to the LEGO beam on the axle and by adding extra support to the axle. If the axle has more than one support, the amount of force being applied to the points where the axle contacts the chassis are lessened. Also, moving the supports further away from each other will also lessen the amount of force and reduce the amount of friction being applied to the axles when they turn, as shown in Figure 3–3.

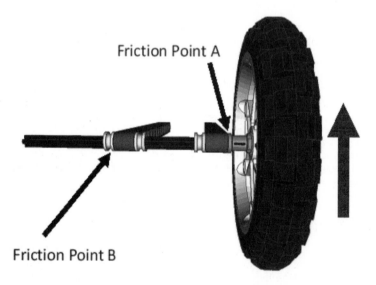

Figure 3–3. By adding an extra support location on the chassis and moving friction point B futher away from friction point A, we reduce the amount of friction being applied to the axle, because we increased the amount of support fo the axle and wheel.

Instead of using a cantilever wheel support system, your robot can use a supported wheel system where the axle is supported on both sides of the wheel, as shown in Figure 3–4. This not only reduces the friction on the axle when it turns but helps keep the wheel straight and even. If the wheel has too much flex, it can give various results over time when traveling. The idea is to remain consistent, so reducing chances in the wheel chamber changing is always a good thing.

Figure 3–4. With the axle and wheel supported evenly on both ends, the friction is reduced drasticly, and you get a much stabler drive system for the robot.

I know of one team that had a very heavy robot whose wheels were supported using a cantilever system, and as the robot sat still resting its full weight on the wheels, the axles started to bend. Over time, this became a big issue, because the robot's performance was constantly changing. Finally, the team realized what was happening and built a stand for the robot to sit on when it wasn't being run, thus taking the weight off the wheels and axles.

Be aware of the friction on your axles; keep them properly supported, and always double-check them before any robot runs. It's very easy for wheels or bushing to get pressed tight accidently and cause unnecessary friction for your wheels.

Programming to Go Straight

Within NXT-G, there are two blocks you can use for moving your robot in a straight line, the Move block and the Motor block. If you have moves or sequences of moves that you wish to repeat in a program, you can collect those sequences in what is called My Block. The following subsections go into more detail.

Both Move and Motor blocks measure rotation in degrees. There are 360 degrees in a circle, or in one rotation. If you want, say, 12 rotations then specify 12 times 360, or 4,320 degrees.

■ **Note** While you can specify a single degree of precision for a rotation, be aware that the motors are not capable of accurately moving by such precise amounts. Don't be fooled into believing that just because you specify a single degree of rotation that you will, in fact, get exactly one degree.

Move Block

The Move block (see Figure 3–5) in NXT-G would seem to be the obvious solution to programming a robot to travel forward straight, and in most cases, this is true. The Move block allows you to control two motors at once and is designed to keep the rotation of the two motors in sync using an internal motor synchronization algorithm. This algorithm works well on most robot designs and shouldn't be a problem.

One of the things missing from the Move block is the ability to control the power ramping for the motors. For example, if you tell your robot to move forward eight rotations with a power setting of 70 percent, it will run at 70 percent power until it gets close to the end of the eighth rotation; then, it will slow down to avoid overshooting its stopping point. With the Move block, you have no control over this ramping down. *Ramping down* is where the Move block slows down the servo as the motor gets closer to the desired duration to avoid overshooting the stopping point. If ramping down poses a problem for what you are trying to accomplish, consider using the Motor block instead.

Also avoid putting a Move block with in a repeating loop; this can cause issues with the Move block maintaining a straight line. The internal logic in the Move block is trying to keep the two motors in sync by tracking their movements, but in a loop, this logic keeps getting reset and can cause confusion for the code.

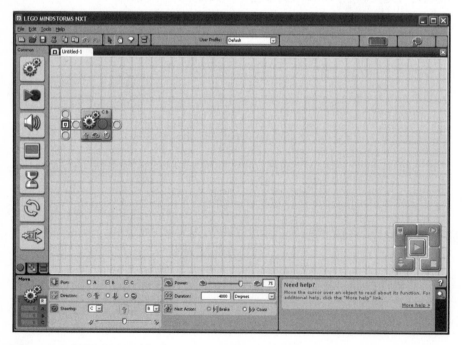

Figure 3–5. NXT-G Move block set to go straight for 4,000 degrees

Motor Block

The Motor block allows you to control only one motor per block, so to go straight with a two-motor–drive robot (a differential drive system), you would need to include two Motor blocks for each section of code that wishes to move the robot forward in a straight line. It will be important that you keep the two blocks in sync yourself.

For example, if you wish for the robot to travel 5,000 degrees forward, you will have to set the distance units on both Motor blocks to be the same. Also, you will need to tell the first of the two Motor blocks to not wait for completion before running the next block by disabling the Wait for Completion checkbox, as shown in Figure 3–6. However, the second block will need the Wait for Completion checkbox enabled. If you fail to do this, the first Motor block will run until the desired duration is met before running the second Motor block, which will cause you robot to spin instead of going straight.

Unlike the Move block, the Motor block will allow you to specify some ramping up or ramping down, but again, you don't have any control over how much power is ramped up or down, nor can you control the duration of the ramping. With the Action parameter in the Move block, you can specify if you want the power of the motor to be ramped up or down when moving. For example, if you set Action to Ramp Up and Power to 80, the motor would not start instantly at a power of 80 but would take a few moments to slowly come up to the desired power level of 80. This can be helpful when trying to avoid tire spin for a robot just starting out from a location, such as base. The amount of ramping is still not within your control and is calculated by the Motor block. If you leave the Action parameter at Constant, the power level is always the same for the motor.

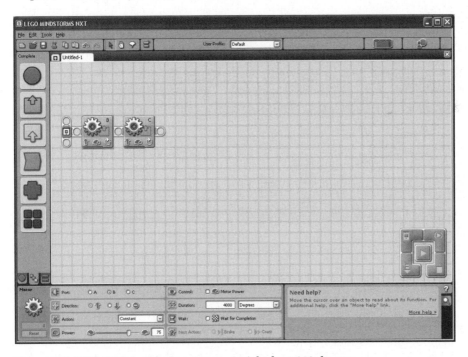

Figure 3–6. NXT-G Motor blocks set to go straight for 4,000 degrees

Reset Motor Block

One of the more underused blocks is the Reset Motor block. Resetting your motors is a great way to help your robot avoid getting confused when running multiple program segments. The block will reset a motor's automatic synchronization that is used in blocks like Move.

It's a safe idea to reset the motors between moves. If your robot seems to get confused about how far it's traveling after running various segments in your program, using the Reset Motor block between these code segments is a great way to keep things running smoothly. Figure 3–7 shows a series of moves separated by motor resets.

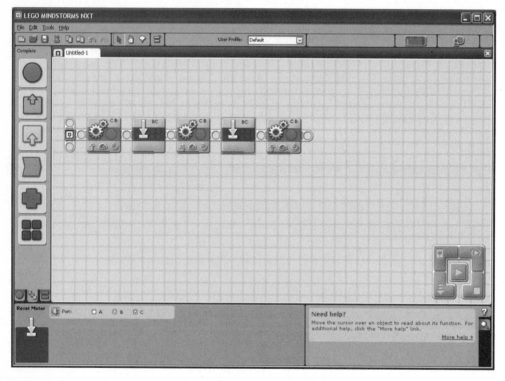

Figure 3–7. A series of move segments with a Reset Motor block between each

Custom MyMove Block

My Block components in NXT-G are simply subprograms that you can create and reuse throughout your programs. Not only do they give you the ease of reusability but they make global changes much easier as well. Say, for example, you have an attachment motor hooked to port A and you commonly make it move up 85 degrees to move your claw attachment. Say you do this in six different programs in your robot. Now, assume you make a change in your attachment, and the claw motor now needs to move 95 degrees each time. You must now make that change in six different programs, but if you had made the claw movement into a My Block, you'd have to change it in only one location, and all the other programs would pick up on that change as soon as the new My Block was loaded.

■ **Note** It is not necessary to use My Block components. However, mastering their use allows your team to create efficient programs that can be adapted to changes faster. They also make the code of your programs much more consistent and readable.

With what you learned earlier, we can create our own custom block for our robot's movements; let's call it a MyMove block. One of the things we talked about earlier was using the circumference of our robot wheels and the desired distance to travel to figure out the number of rotations our motor needed to turn. To make life simpler, we could add that math into a MyMove block and have the NXT figure out the necessary rotations for you.

In Figure 3–8, you can see that I have created three variables, Motor Power, Circumference, and Distance. If we use these variables, the Motor Power variable will feed directly into our Move block's power wire. The Circumference and Distance will feed into a Math Block, so we can divide the Distance value by the Circumference to get the necessary rotations for the motor to reach our destination.

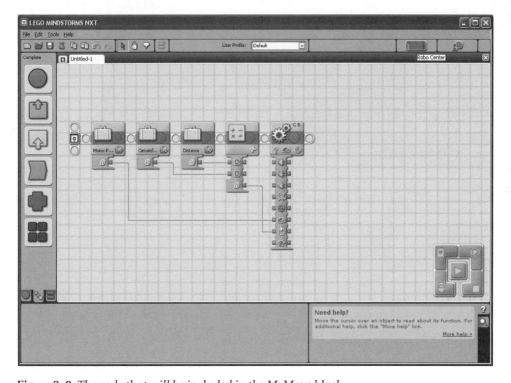

Figure 3–8. The code that will be included in the MyMove block

Now that we have our code, we can create the MyMove block. When creating a My Block that has parameters, you need to be careful when selecting the code that will be included in the actual block and leave out of the selection the variables that will be the parameters, as shown in Figure 3–9.

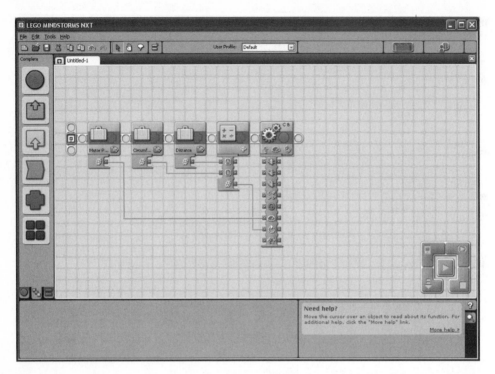

Figure 3–9. *Highlighting just the Math and Move block, the variables are left out so that they will become parameters for our MyMove block.*

Now that we have the Math and Move blocks selected, we can create the MyMove My Block. As you can see in Figure 3–6, when I created the MyMove block, there are three # signs on the left. These represent the three variables that I was using for inputs. They will now show as parameters for the MyMove block, as you can see in Figures 3–10 and 3–11.

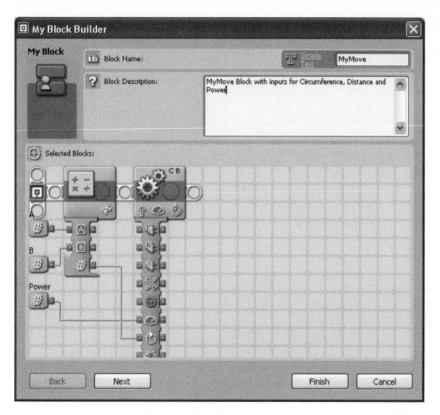

Figure 3–10. The new code that will be included in the MyMove block, including three input parameters.

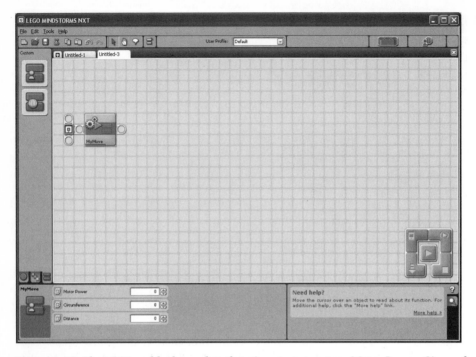

Figure 3–11. *The MyMove block now has three input parameters, Motor Power, Circumference, and*
Distance.

Now, we have a reusable MyMove block that can be used in place of a Move block, and the nice
thing is that it will calculate the number of rotations needed based on the information you provide to it.

You can build on this and make a MyMove block just for your one particular robot. Then, you could
hard-code the circumference of your robot's wheels into the MyMove block with a Constant block and
only have to enter the Distance and Motor power when using the MyMove block, as shown in Figure 3–
12. That way, if you changed the wheels on your robot, you'd only have to make the change to the
circumference value in your MyMove block to match your new wheel size, and all the programs that use
this block would change accordingly—very simple with no mess.

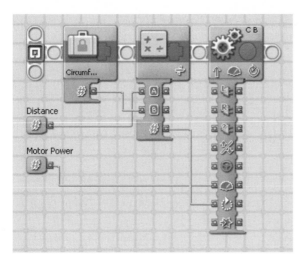

Figure 3–12. This MyMove block has only two inputs; the Circumference is stored in a Constant block.

Batteries

With NXT, there are two basic battery power options: the NXT rechargeable battery pack and 6 AA batteries. Both of these can have an effect on your robots ability to go straight and the reach the desired position.

Replaceable Batteries

In the early days of LEGO MINDSTORMS, the original RCX used only AA batteries. You could use rechargeable batteries, but there wasn't a rechargeable battery pack available like the current NXT has. Before the built-in rotation sensors, like in the NXT servos, many teams would try to use time as a unit for navigating straight, but they soon found out that time is a horrible unit of measurement to use for moving, and AA batteries it made it even worse. Since the motors run differently based on the battery power level, the robot was completely unpredictable. The results changed as the batteries drained.

When using odometry for navigation, using some unit of distance as the duration is going to be your best bet to avoid differences based on high or low battery power levels. The number of rotations represents a better, or at least more repeatable, measure of distance than time. Using time for duration just doesn't deliver consistent results, and consistency is the goal.

If you choose to use regular or even rechargeable AA batteries, keep in mind that you will need to design your robot in such a way that you can quickly change out the batteries. Also, you will need to bring plenty of extra batteries with you to the competition. Even though an FLL meet is only 2.5 minutes long, you still need battery power for testing and practice runs plus any technical demonstrations you need to do for the judges.

Rechargeable Battery Packs

The NXT rechargeable battery pack will give your robot a much more consistent source of power, thus giving your more predictably when completing task. The interesting thing to note is that the NXT rechargeable battery pack only outputs slightly less than 8 volts, while with normal AA batteries, the initial output is around 9 volts. The key is that the AA batteries will drop in output power over time, but the rechargeable battery pack power level stays very consistent over the life of the charge. There is a drop off in power as the rechargeable battery pack comes to the end of its charge, but overall, it stays pretty even with its output levels.

■ **Note** As you can imagine, having a constant output level is going to benefit your robot much more than having the higher power level for a limited about of time.

If you use the NXT rechargeable battery pack, remember to build your robot in such a way that you have easy access to the recharging plug on the battery pack and so that you can see the indicator lights. One year, my team could not see the indicator lights on the battery pack, so after charging the battery overnight, we found that we had not plugged up the battery charger plug completely so it never received a charge. This became very obvious the next morning at an FLL scrimmage when our robot failed to power up at the event. The robot design was changed so that the red and green indicator lights on the NXT rechargeable battery pack could easily be seen in the future.

Helpers

Your robot doesn't just have to depend on its motors and wheels for going straight. Just as a carpenter can use several tools to ensure a straight cut, your robot can use and incorporate helper tools as well. These can be additions to your actual robot or something you've built to help the robot while it's in base. Don't be afraid to take advantage of such helpers; whatever you can do to keep your robot consistent is going to help you win.

Wall Following

Even the best-designed robots have trouble going perfectly straight for a long distance on a game field. There are just too many variables that can affect the robot's ability to drive in a perfectly straight line, but there are other ways to handle long-distance straight driving.

On an FLL game field, the table is made up of 2×4 lumber, which serves as the walls around the field. Take advantage of these walls; they can be very useful in robot navigation. The simplest use of the walls is *wall following*. The basic idea is to run your robot along the wall using some kind of guide wheels on your robot chassis.

When you evaluate your missions, you will find that some of them are on the far end of the game field and will require to you to travel a long distance to reach the task. Look at the game field and find out if there is a wall that is free of obstacles. If so, this wall can become your friend in making those long runs. If there is something in the way, you may be able to move it out of the way, but be sure to verify this with the rules of the game.

To use wall following, you simply mount a set of small wheels on the side of your chassis, with the wheels mounted perpendicular to the game field. These wheels will most likely have no tires mounted on them; you can use just the plastic wheels. Since they are being used as guides, we don't need them to get any real traction.

You can see a set of wall following wheels that I have attached to my DemoBot in Figures 3–13 and 3–14. Now, you program your robot to run forward with a very slight turn into the wall so that the robot will run along the wall. Don't overdo the turn into the wall; there's no need to make a lot of extra work for your robot by causing too much friction between the robot and the wall. You want to turn just enough that the robot will use the wall as a guide.

Figure 3–13. A pair of simple wall follower wheels to be used on DemoBot

When approaching the wall, keep the angle small, around 30 degrees or less; hitting the wall going straight with a 45-degree or higher angle could cause the robot turn the wrong way and possibly get the robot stuck, as Figure 3–15 illustrates. Figure 3–16 shows a robot hitting a wall at a more reasonable angle. Figure 3–17 shows how the robot then tracks accurately along the wall.

Your guide wheels should not be too small either; it is possible the wood at your competition may not be perfect and could have some minor knots or chips. You don't want tiny wheels to cause your robot to get stuck while running down the wall.

The guide wheels should have plenty of clearance for the robot to turn into the wall without the chassis of the robot making contact before the guide wheels do, so place the wheels far enough apart that they makes smooth contact with the wall when your robot makes a connection with it.

Also, don't put your guide wheels up to high; keep them in the middle of the wall height if possible. If they're too low, the robot could bend or twist the guides; too high and the guides can get caught on the top of the walls. This happened to one of my teams; the walls on the event table were just a tiny bit shorter than our practice table, so when the robot went to make contact with the wall, the guide wheels caught the top edge of the table wall and caused the robot to get stuck.

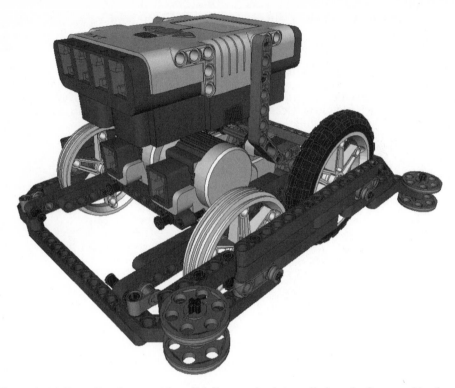

Figure 3–14. DemoBot shown with wall follower wheels installed on the front and back

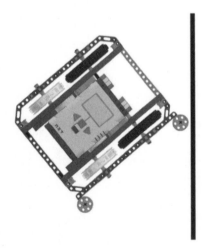

Figure 3–15 *This approach angle is too sharp to begin wall following; coming in this sharply could cause the robot to pivot the wrong direction and get stuck.*

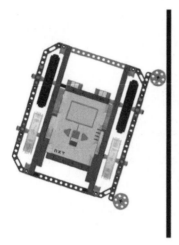

Figure 3–16. An approach angle like this will make for a smooth transition to following the wall.

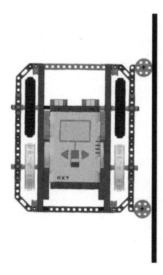

Figure 3–17. Once your robot is agaisnt the wall, the front guide wheel will be making the most contact with the wall, since the program will be telling your robot to turn slightly into the wall while running down the walls surface.

If your practice table is not painted but your event tables are (most likely they will have paint on the walls), this could affect your robot's performance at the competition. Try to make your practice table as much like the event tables as you can. Even something simple as painted walls could change the way your robot performs at practice versus at the events.

I have seen teams try to use the NXT Ultrasonic sensor to achieve wall following, but this rarely gave consistent results and actually registered improperly at times, causing the robot to not follow the wall at all. I personally wouldn't recommend using the sensor for this function, but I won't discourage a team from trying something new.

Base Jigs

I am not a fan of point-and-shoot robots. To use a *point-and-shoot robot*, you point the robot in a particular direction in base, set the rotations of the motors, and then just let it go hoping it hits the target. However, if you must do some kind of aiming from base toward a particular area on the field, building a jig to use in your base is valid in FLL. A *jig* is a tool that is used to align or hold the robot in place before it leaves base. If you decide to build a jig to help guide your robot in the right direction, it must be made completely out of LEGO elements.

The idea is that your robot is required to start from a particular point in order for it to reach its goal, and it's critical that the robot start in the exact same place each time. No matter how much your team tries, you will rarely achieve this goal with just using your eyes. So using the walls in base as a reference is a good idea, and you can build a jig that fits in base to help position your robot for your mission start.

To use a jig, you need to find some kind of reference point when placing the jig so that you know it's in the right place each time. Most likely, one of the walls in base will be helpful; if you're lucky, you have two walls in base. Be careful, though, that the field mat is in the same position as well. In the FLL Smart Moves game, the mat was centered in the table, so the gap between the wall and base varied on different tables. In that case, using this part of the wall in base was not as helpful when distance was being measured off the wall, but it was still useful for keeping the robot square before exiting base.

In FLL competitions, the jig can only be used in the base and must be removed after the robot leaves the base. The jig is strictly a tool being used by the team and can have no effect on the mission results. And again, just like everything else, the jig must be made of only LEGO parts.

Tips

If you ask any experienced LEGO robotics teams, they will most likely tell you come cool tips they have learned over the years for improving their robots' navigation and performance—don't be afraid to ask. Many teams love sharing what they have learned; that is one of the great things about LEGO robotics. A few of the tips my teams have learned over the years are simple but have become very effective in helping our robots perform.

Motor Matching

Believe it or not, all LEGO NXT servo motors are not alike. For the most part, they are very consistent, but I have found motors that run completely differently from each other. Some wear out faster than others; some get abused or misused. In a classroom where various students have been using the robots over the years, many of the motors can be out of sync and not running as well as some of the other motors in your collection.

If you have only the three motors that came in your LEGO MINDSTORMS kit, motor matching might not be a big deal for you, since it will be fairly easy for you to figure out if one of the motors is not performing as well as the others. But if you have multiple kits and an assortment of motors, a little motor matching could be helpful.

The idea behind motor matching is to find two motors that are compatible with each other; you'd like to find two motors that run at the same pace, start evenly, and brake at the same time. These matched motors will then be used as your drive motors. Once they are matched, mark them somehow, either with a temporary sticker (or tape) or even a colored TECHNIC peg; just don't use anything permanent since FLL rules doesn't allow any extra marking on your LEGO elements.

When matching motors, I have built a simple machine that the motors will rest in and run a set of gears. By running the same simple program on each pair of motors, I can keep switching out various motors until I find two that work well together. I set them aside and then match up the next pair. The motor matching machine is shown in Figure 3–17, and the NXT-G program to test the motors is in Figure 3–18.

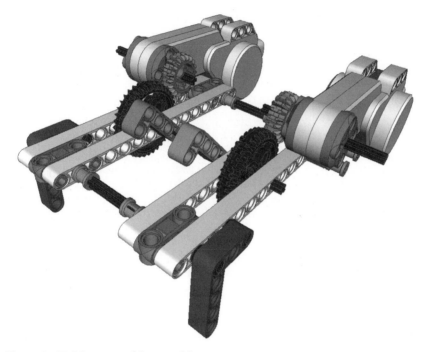

Figure 3–17. Motor matching machine

The program is very simple. It just runs the motors forward for 30 rotations, breaks, and then runs backward another 30 rotations and breaks. If the gears for both motors are in the same position, you know they are compatible. No two motors may be exact, but you just want to pair up the closes ones that you can.

Figure 3–18. This motor matching machine NXT-G program runs the motors forward, stops, resets motors, plays a tone, and then runs the motors backward.

Removing Gear Slack

You may have noticed that there is a bit of backlash or gear slack in the NXT servo motor, more so if you've added gearing to your robot's drive train. This is normal and to be expected. Even though we're working with some very impressive robot tools, they are still LEGO robots and have certain limitations when it comes to keeping things tight and precisely lined up. If the gears are too tight, they will bind when turning, but if they are too loose, you end up with a lot of slack in the gears and slipping. However, even when we find the happy medium between the two, there is still going to be some expected play in the gears that will allow our axles and wheels to turn some before the gears mesh up.

This gear slack can be an issue for going straight at times when one drive wheel has more slack in the gears than the other side. Obviously, this disparity can cause the robot make a slight turn when it first starts out. Or our odometry results can be affected if the slack is too great.

One trick I've learned from teams over the years is to get your robot a very slight push when sitting in base, just roll the robot forward a small bit forcing the wheels to turn the NXT Servo and mesh up the gears. It's easy to forget to do this during a stressful competition, but if you practice it as part of your regular routine, it will quickly become second nature to do it when ever your running your robot.

Troubleshooting

When a robot stops running straight, first ask yourself what has changed. Did something on the robot change, either on purpose or by accident? Take the time to thoroughly check over the robot and verify that everything is still snapped tight.

Next, check the tires for wear or to ensure that they are mounted properly on the wheel. Some LEGO tires need a little help to sit properly on the LEGO wheel. If one tire is mounted poorly, this can cause the robot to track in the wrong direction. You wouldn't think that tire wear could be an issue, but after months of practicing, the rubber on the LEGO tires can wear down and cause issues. If you see problems with going straight, check out the tires before making any program changes.

Think about any kind of weight changes on the robot as well. Did an attachment get added that caused the robot to get heavier?

Also be sure that when someone says "the robot isn't going straight" that that doesn't really mean "the robot isn't going where I want it to go." There is a big difference. Many times, a team will struggle with starting the robot in exactly the same spot in base each time and then blame the difference in final location on the actual robot and not the operator. I've spent many team meetings explaining that the robot only does what it's told to do and it's not broken when it does something you didn't expect or want. Inconsistent aiming of the robot tends to cause many false alarms in regards to defective robot chassis or programs.

Does the robot make a quick jerk or direction change when it starts moving before going straight? If so, make sure your robot is stable and balanced properly. If you have four wheels and only three are touching the field when the robot is at rest, this can cause conditions that will shift the robot's starting direction.

When you do make changes to the robot or program, make changes one at a time and then test your robot. Never make more than one drastic change at one time. And spend a lot of time observing what the robot is doing each time. Run it multiple times over and over just to watch it fail and study what the robot is doing. I know it's hard to do this at times because you just want to fix the robot, but you will learn so much about how to fix it once you fully understand what is broken.

Summary

As you can see, there are multiple variables that can affect if you robot travels straight or not. In the end, these are LEGO robots, so their accuracy will never be 100 percent, but following the ideas shared in this chapter should help straighten out your robot's path considerably. If you robot continues to navigate in a direction you didn't expect, slow it down some and run it over and over again studying its every motion. By doing so, you might see something you didn't see before, and that something could be the difference between a robot that navigates straight and one that doesn't.

■ ■ ■

CHAPTER 4

Consistent Turning

There was a great movie back in the 1980s that had a character giving his buddy tips on how to ski; his simple instructions were, "Go that way, really fast. If something gets in your way, turn." Well, that advice can apply to robots too. We want our robots to go toward the mission, and if an obstacle gets in our way, we're going to need to turn. The trick is turning in a consistent manner that allows our robot to end up where we expect it to.

There are just as many factors that affect a smooth turn as for going straight. Your robot's wheels, chassis design, and of course, programming all play a big part in turning smoothly.

■ **Tip** When going straight, having a robot that with a low center of gravity is helpful. The same is true when turning. If the robot chassis is top heavy or off balance, a quick turn could cause the robot to flip over on its side. Even a robot that tilts a little due to loss of balance when turning would cause undesired turning accuracy. If the drive wheels lose contact with the field at any time during a turn, making an accurate turn will be impossible. We want consistent and accurate turns, so keep the robot on the ground at all times. Keep the chassis balanced, and turn slowly to avoid losing wheel contact.

Turning Designs

There are basically two types of turning method designs used on LEGO robots, and really only one of them is desirable when building an FLL robot. There are differential steering drive systems and steering drive systems. The latter is rarely used in FLL robots because it's too complex and difficult to pull off with a LEGO MINDSTORM robot. I do think steering system robots have their place and are a great challenge to build, but when it comes to building a winning FLL robot, the differential steering system is hard to beat for its simplicity and ease of use.

Differential Steering Systems

A *differential steering robot*, also called a *differentially steered drive system*, is one of the most common steering systems used on small robots and works well for LEGO robots. Differential steering is very simple and easy to create with LEGO, and it works much like the drive system of a wheelchair. Each axle is independently controlled for driving and steering, thus allowing the axles to move at different speeds and directions. This allows the robot to turn based solely on applying varying power to the motors. So, like a wheelchair, if you turn one wheel forward and one in reverse, the chair will spin in place (assuming you turn both wheels at the same rate and degrees of rotation). Also if you spin only one wheel, the chair will rotate in a circle using the stationary wheel as the pivot point. And if you turn both wheels in the same direction but at different speeds, the chair will turn in a curved path towards the slower wheel. Being able to turn in such a way allows a robot to make quick steering changes with a minimum of space. The DemoBot (see Figure 4–1) uses differential steering for making turns.

If you notice on the DemoBot, the rear wheels do not have tires, because when the front tires are rotating and making the robot turn, the rear wheels are going to skid across the surface. The rear wheels do not need to get traction; they are simply there to help balance the robot. If the robot was using a caster wheel on the back, that wheel would simply turn passively with the robot as it rotated. You can even have skids on the back, as we discussed in Chapter 2. Whatever design you use, make sure it does not create a lot of friction when the robot starts to turn. The trick is to make the turn as frictionless as possible, so that we get a nice smooth turn. If the robot stumbles or encounters too much friction with the field, our turning accuracy will be diminished considerably.

Be careful to not confuse differential steering with the differential drive system used on automobiles; a differential drive system is where a single source of power is delivered to the drive wheels through a differential gear system. This is not the same as having two independent power sources for the robot's drive wheels. Sometimes, the similar terminology confuses people.

Figure 4–1. *DemoBot is an example of a differential steering robot chassis design. The two motors are used to control the speed as well as the direction.*

DIFFERENTIAL GEAR SYSTEMS

A *differential gear system* ideally evenly applies torque to two outputs, such as axles, and allows the output axles to turn at different rates.

The trick to a differential gear system is that the two output axles are allowed to turn at different rates if needed. This is important when making a turn. Imagine having a pair of wheels locked to a single axle in such a way that they must always turn at the same rate. Now, if this pair of wheels is driven into a turn, the wheels will have a hard time completing the turn, since each wheel needs to travel a different distance. The wheel on the inside of the turn needs to turn less than the wheel on the outside of the turn. The inside wheel would actually drag some when turning, thus requiring the power source to create more power to overcome the friction caused by the dragging wheel.

Having a differential gear system with wheels that can turn at a different rate will avoid this problem and make for a smooth turn. Most modern rear-wheel drive cars and trucks make use of a differential on their real wheels.

Steering Drive Systems

A *steering drive system* is what most cars use to turn; in a robot, you would have a single motor powering the robot and then a second motor controlling the steering. You would most likely have a differential gear system on the drive wheels to prevent skidding and some kind of rack system on the front steering mechanism. With LEGO robots, systems like this can be a bit more difficult to build but can be done with a little patience.

There are multiple variations for a steering drive robot. You can have two wheels that turn, like on a car, or have a single steering wheel that controls the steering. When having two wheels that steer, you have to be concerned about wheel skid, since both steering wheels are pivoting on their own pivot points and not on a common point. Cars overcome this problem by using Ackerman steering correction. This is a geometry that reduces the skid of the wheels by forcing the steering wheels to turn along the same steering arc. Without Ackerman correction, the steering wheels will turn on different steering arcs, forcing them to skid and throw off your robot's odometry calculations. A single steering wheel such as on a tricycle will prevent this problem, since you then only have to deal with a single turning arc instead of two.

The advantage to a steering drive system is that you have separated the drive system from the steering system, so you no longer have to worry about issues like motor matching and keeping two motors' rotations in sync. This is great for situations in which you're using odometry.

A disadvantage to using steering drive is that turning into tight spots is not as easy as it is with a differential steering system. A differential steering system has a zero turning radius, while a steering drive robot must move some distance as it turns. As with a car, you can turn the steer wheels all you want, but a robot with a steering drive system won't actually start to turn until it moves either forward or backward. You'll see many lawn tractors that now use a zero turn radius system so they can get into tight spots when cutting a lawn, versus a traditional lawn tractor that might have to back up and make multiple attempts to reach a hard-to-access patch of grass.

One of the biggest disadvantages that I have found with steering drive robots is that when a robot is running in autonomous mode, such as FLL robots, it's very hard to keep track of when the robot is pointed straight. Even with the built-in rotation sensors in the NXT servos, you still can never be 100 percent sure that the robot's steering is tracking straight. If the robot is remote controlled, it's easy for the human operator to adjust the steering back to straight, but it's a much larger task with autonomous LEGO robots. I have never seen any real benefits of going with such a design in a LEGO robots competition such as FLL.

Calculating Turns

There are two different ways to turn a differential steering robot: by turning both wheels or by only turning one wheel and pivoting on the stationary wheel. The trick is to figure out how much you should turn the wheel to get the desired turning position.

Bear in mind that, while we can accurate calculate the proper degrees needed for a precision turn, we are still dealing with LEGO robots that are not precision machines. No matter how accurate your math, any LEGO robot that you build will still need some final tweaking.

■ **Note:** There is about six to eight degrees of gear slack in a LEGO NXT servo, so getting accurate movements down within a few degrees will not be possible. Always allow some room for error when turning.

Single-Wheel Turns

In a *single-wheel turn*, one wheel remains stationary while the other moves and controls the turn. If you are turning your robot to the right by only turning the right wheel forward and keeping the left wheel stationary, this will create a steering circle with the left wheel position as the center (pivot point), and the distance between the right and left wheel, called the *track*, will be the radius of the steering circle, as shown in Figure 4–2. The circumference of the steering circle is calculated with the following formula:

Circumference = 2 × radius × pi

To turn 90 degrees, our robot would have to travel one-fourth of the circumference of the steering circle, while a 180-degree turn would require traveling half the steering circle circumference. Therefore, to calculate the desired duration needed to use in our Motor block, we first figure out the distance we need to travel around our steering circle. If we're turning 360 degrees (a complete circle) with our DemoBot, which has a has a track of 5 inches, the equation would be something like this:

Distance = Steering circle circumference
Distance = 2 × 5 × 3.14
Distance = 31.4 inches

With the distance now known, we can calculate the duration needed in our Motor block by using the same formula that we used to calculate the duration when going straight. Our robot has wheels that have a diameter of 3.25 inches, so the calculation will look like this:

Duration = Distance / Wheel circumference
Duration = 31.4 / (3.25 × 3.14)
Duration = 2.86 rotations

The value 2.86 gives us the rotation duration needed to turn the robot a single degree, for the robot to make a complete circle we would multiply 360 by the single degree number (2.86).

Duration = 2.86 rotations × 360 degrees
Duration = 1029.6 degrees

Now, we have found that the number 2.86 is the key. We can multiply this number by any angle turn we wish to make. If we want our robot to turn 90 degrees instead of 360, we simply calculate the duration by using our new-found key of 2.86. The duration for a 90-degree turn is figured like such:

Duration = 2.86 × 90
Duration = 257.4 degrees

Even though our key value is unitless, remember when making these calculations that you keep the units the same for your other values, so if you're measuring your track in inches, the resulting distance will also be in inches. This is the same for the wheel diameter; if all your other measurements are in inches, you need to measure the wheel in inches as well. Mixing English measurements with metric measurements can cause disastrous results.

■ **Note** One of the most famous of all metric versus English mix-ups resulted in the loss of the Mars Climate Orbiter that was part of NASA's Mars Surveyor '98 program. That spacecraft was destroyed due to a navigation error induced by using metric values where English values (that is, Imperial System, or IS, values) were expected. You can read more about the story at `http://en.wikipedia.org/wiki/Mars_Climate_Orbiter`.

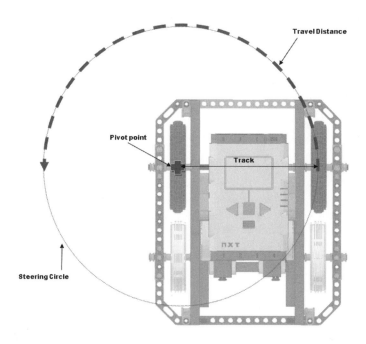

Figure 4–2. DemoBot making a 180-degree turn with a single motor would create a steering circle with the diameter being twice that of the robot's track. The track is the distance between the robot's drive wheels. The center of the steering circle would be the point at which the robot would pivot on the nonmoving wheel.

Dual-Wheel Pivot

With the single-wheel turn, our robot is only powering one wheel and turns the robot around an arc. But if we turn both wheels in opposite directions, we can pivot the robot right where it is sitting. The pivot point is no longer the stationary wheel but the center of the robot's track. We can even calculate the number of degrees needed to make the turn in the same way that we did with the single-wheel turn. The only difference is that we will have to divide the degrees in half and apply them to both wheels—and remember that one wheel will be going in the opposite direction of the other. In Figure 4–3, you can see that the steering circle is much smaller than the steering circle of a single wheel turn, actually half the size.

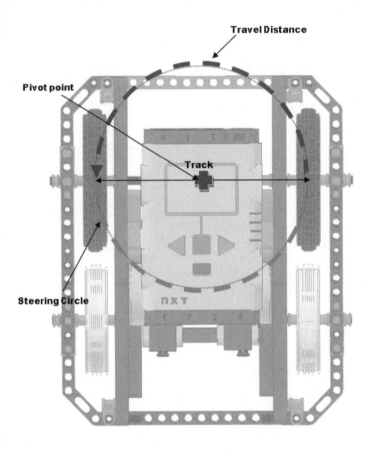

Figure 4–3. DemoBot making a 180-degree pivot turn with both motors would create a steering circle with the diameter equal to the length of the robot's track. The center of the steering cirlce would be the center point of the robot track.

Say we want to pivot our DemoBot 180 degrees. We again use our key value of 2.86 that we calculated earlier. This time, we multiply it by 180 and then divide by 2:

Pivot duration = (2.86 × 180) / 2
Pivot duration = 514.8 / 2
Pivot duration = 257.4 degrees

If we are using a Move block, we set the steering to 100 or –100, depending on which direction we wish to turn, and then enter a duration of 257.4 degrees, as shown in Figure 4–4.

We can also use a pair of Motor blocks, one for motor B and one for motor C. Simply set the duration for both Motor blocks to 257.4 degrees, and set one Motor block to travel in the opposite direction of the other. Be sure to either put the blocks in parallel or set up the first block so it does not wait for completion, or else NXT will run the first Motor block and then run the second one, giving you a completely different turn result than you expected (see Figure 4–5).

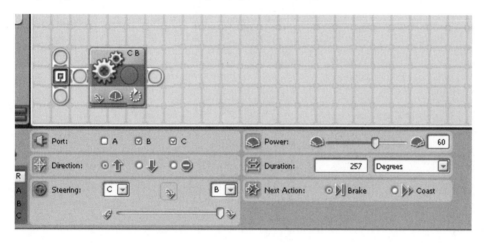

Figure 4–4. A Move block being set to pivot the DemoBot 180 degrees by using the value of 257.4 as the Duration and the steering set to the far right.

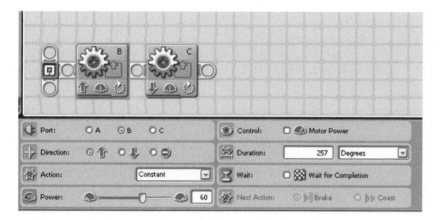

Figure 4–5. Two Motor blocks being set to pivot the DemoBot 180 degrees by using the value of 257.4 as the Duration and turning the two blocks in opposite directions.

Both the Move and Motor blocks work equally well for pivoting. I have always preferred the pairing of the two Motor blocks versus using the Move block. However, that is just my personal preference.

Programming

I've already mentioned that you can choose between Move and Motor blocks when turning. You can also create custom blocks using the My Block builder. The following subsections show how to program these different choices.

Move Block

We talked about the Move block for use when we wanted to go straight. Now that we want to turn, the Move block can be used again. The Move block has a steering parameter that allows for values between –100 and 100. A slider on the block can move 10 positions to the right and 10 positions to the left, and each position represents increments of 10. If you wish to enter a value that is not an increment of 10, you can simply pass it in via the wired parameter.

The key values that are helpful with using the Move block for steering are in Table 4–1.

Table 4–1. Move block common steering settings

Steering Value	Steering Results
100	Pivot to the right
50	Turn to the right using one motor
0	Go straight
−50	Turn to the left using one motor
−100	Pivot to the left

Other steering values are allowed and can be useful when you want to travel in a large arc, but these require a bit more trial and error when using the Move block. It is a good idea to keep the speed in the 25–75 range; going too fast or too slow adds some unexpected results to the Move block steering at times.

Motor Blocks

I have always preferred to have my teams use the Motor blocks when making turns. The results can be much more predictable because you are controlling each motor separately; you have the ability to get a bit more precision with the values that you can apply to the motors. Using a Motor block for each motor lets you apply different power values, as well as adjust the duration values differently as well. This can be helpful when trying to match a particular trajectory arc. At the same time, teams new to NXT-G sometimes get confused by switching between Move and Motor blocks. If you're more comfortable with using just the Move blocks, do what works best for you and your team.

With the Motor blocks, you will find that you have more control over your turns simply because you specify the actual power and duration for each motor. As you saw earlier when calculating the durations for our various types of turns, it's nice to have this kind of control over each motor.

If I was trying to move my robot along a large trajectory using arcs, the Motor blocks would give me the ability navigate such an arc with a lot more predictability.

One of the tricks is to remember that these Motor blocks need to be run in sequence either by branching off a second tread or by setting the first Motor block in the sequence with the Wait for Completion checkbox unselected. Also, be aware that one Motor block may complete before the other, so you will need to let both motor blocks finish before your code moves on to the next statement. By simply adding a slight delay after your move, you can compensate for this 90 percent of the time. If you need something more complex, you can simply add some logic that confirms both Motor blocks have completed their movements before advancing to the next statement in your program.

Creating a Custom MyPivot Block

As you learned in Chapter 3, we can create our own custom programming blocks in NXT-G by using My Block components, which allow us to take some of our own code and combine it into a useable block of code that we can share among many different programs. Code reusability is great for saving time and memory in our NXT brick. Also, including custom My Block components in your code is one of the things that technical judges will be looking for during any kind of technical interview with your team. Be sure to talk about any custom blocks you create and make sure everyone on the team understands what they do.

While doing all the calculations for figuring out the correct duration needed to turn in the direction we desire, you may have realized that much of that logic could be included in a custom My Block to be used for making a pivot turn; let's call that new block MyPivot.

For example, once we know the key value, 2.86 for the DemoBot, we could make that a constant in our new MyPivot block. Then, all we need to do is enter the desired turning degrees and let the block calculate the true duration needed for our robot to complete the turn.

If our robot's wheels or track size change in the future, we simply recalculate the key value and modify the key constant in our MyPivot block without needing to modify any of our code elsewhere. In Figure 4–6, you can see the code that will make up our new MyPivot block. We have a Variable block for our degrees and a Constant block that will hold our key value of 2.86. These values are then passed to the Math block, where they are multiplied by each other and passed to one more Math block so that we can divide them by 2. The new calculated duration is then passed to a pair of Motor blocks that are running in opposite direction of each other.

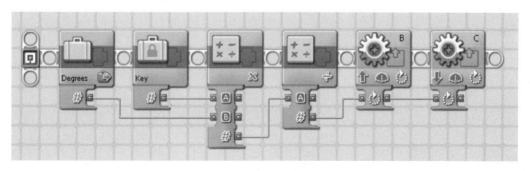

Figure 4–6. The definition of MyPivot block, which will allow us to pass in the desired turn degrees and have the duration calculated automaticly.

Now, to create our new MyPivot block, we will select all the blocks in our code except the Degrees variable; we will purposely leave this block out of our selection (you'll see why in a moment). Once the blocks are selected, as shown in Figure 4–7, go to the Edit menu, and select Make a New My Block. Then, you will see the My Block Builder dialog with the code you selected displayed. Notice that, since we did not select the Variable block that contained our degrees value, a special parameter wire was added to our new block. Currently, this wire is labeled with the letter "B," but we can change that later. Figure 4–8 shows the newly created MyPivot block being used with the single parameter of Degrees.

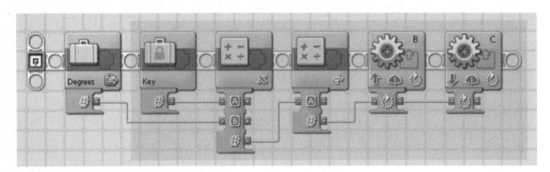

Figure 4–7. *Selected blocks that will be a part of our new MyPivot block*

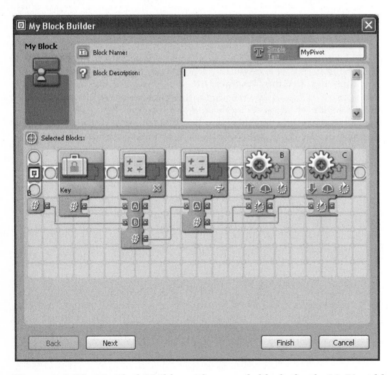

Figure 4–8. *The My Block Builder with our code blocks for the MyPivot block. The wired parameter labeled "B" will be our input of degrees.*

Now, when we're finished in the My Block Builder dialog, our newly created MyPivot block will be inserted into our code and put in place of the code we selected to be part of the block, as shown in Figure 4–9. You'll also notice that, when you select the MyPivot block, you are presented with one single parameter labeled "B." This parameter is the degrees that we want our robot to pivot.

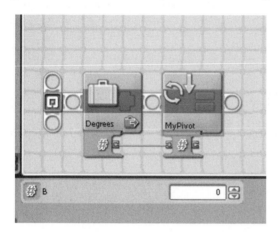

Figure 4–9. Here, you can see the new MyPivot block connected to the Variable block that we left out of the MyPivot defintion.

We could just leave the label set to the letter "B" as long as we remember what the parameter is expecting, but to make the best use of our new MyPivot block, we should add the proper label for our own reusability and to help anyone else on the team who may want to use the MyPivot block.

To change the label, we simply select the MyPivot block and either double-click the block or select the Edit menu and choose Edit Selected My Block. The My Block Builder dialog will open, showing you the code blocks contained within your MyPivot block. If you click the "B" label for the input parameter, you can simply type any new label you wish. In our case, we'll rename the parameter Degrees, as shown in Figure 4–10.

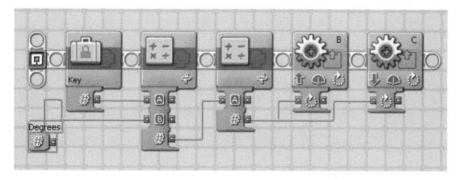

Figure 4–10. Changing the label on the input parameter to say "Degrees" instead of the letter "B."

Now, whenever we use the MyPivot block, the parameter will show up as Degrees and make much more sense to whoever is using the MyPivot block; this helps make the code self-documenting. You can see the results in Figure 4–11.

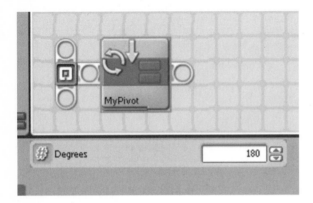

Figure 4–11. *The final MyPivot block with the input parameter properly labeled to make it easy to read and use.*

Creating a Custom MyTurn Block

Say you want a block to do single wheel turns. You can simply modify the MyPivot block by removing one of the Motor blocks and removing the Math block that was dividing the calculated value by 2. The results would look like those shown in Figure 4–12.

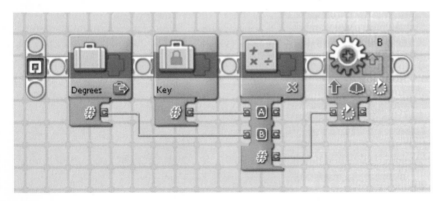

Figure 4–12. *The MyTurn block, simliar to the MyPivot block but with only one Motor block and a single Math block*

Now, if the Move block is more your style for steering but you'd like to have more flexibility with the steering parameter, you could create a MyMoveSteering block that accepts a parameter value between – 100 and 100, thus giving you more control of the steering than using the slider that currently exist in the Move block.

Summary

Steering a LEGO robot is an art at times, but knowing the math behind accurate turning can help get your robot close to where you want it to be. I would never make more than two turns before realigning the robot with some fixture on the game field; we will talk about how to do this in later chapters. Too many unchecked turns in a single run can cause the room for error to expand greatly.

When making a turn with your robot think it through, try not to guess at the duration and angle needed. The more you can understand about why your robot is turning the way that it is the easier it will be for you to make corrections in its turning direction.

■ ■ ■

CHAPTER 5

Line Following and Detection

A smart robot can detect its surroundings and make decisions based on its findings; a smart robot is a winning robot. One of the ways to make your robot smart is by giving it the ability to receive input from the game field. Using a light sensor on your MINDSTORMS robot is a great place to start when adding some intelligence. I have found that many new teams are intimidated by using sensors other than the rotation sensors built into the NXT servos, but this doesn't need to be the case.

One of the great things about the NXT Light sensor is that it's pretty much a passive sensor from a hardware perspective: you simply put it on your robot facing the direction you wish to use for detection and wire it up, and it is ready for action. With that said, you will need to have a good understanding of how the sensor works and what you'll use it for in order to get the most out of it. Also, being able to develop smart programming code to interrupt the input received from the NXT Light sensor will be important.

First, you need a better understanding of what the NXT Light sensor is and how it works. Then, we can talk about how we can make use of it.

NXT Light Sensor

The NXT Light sensor allows your robot to visually analyze its environment, basically giving your robot the gift of sight. It will be able to detect the differences between light and dark, either by detecting the ambient light of its surroundings or by analyzing the color of something in front of the sensor.

The LEGO MINDSTORMS Education NXT Base Set (9797) includes one NXT Light sensor. The retail product LEGO MINDSTORMS 2.0 no longer includes the NXT Light sensor but instead has an NXT Color sensor. The NXT Color Sensor can be used in the same manner as the LEGO Light Sensor so anything in this chapter regarding the Light Sensor also applies to the Color Sensor.

In FLL, you are allowed to use two NXT Light sensors on your robot. One is often enough, but having a second sensor is helpful with some designs. The rules can change each year regarding the rules in FLL so be sure to always refer to the current rule listings each season.

The NXT Light sensor contains an LED and a phototransistor; the phototransistor actually reads the reflected light from the LED or ambient light in the room. The Light sensor ideally is reading from a very narrow field of vision; this field is based on the distance of the sensor from the source. For example, if you were to point the light sensor at the light in your ceiling, you would get a very high-level reading. Now, if you hold a black LEGO brick in between your robot and the ceiling light, the sensor would not recognized the brick simply because the field of vision is too great. However, if you placed the brick on a table and pointed and held the light sensor just a few inches over the brick, it would be able to detect the dark-colored brick. Keep this in mind when placing your Light sensor on your robot's chassis. Don't position your sensor so far away that it cannot distinguish what you want it to.

The NXT Light sensor can read light in two modes: ambient light and reflective light. Ambient light readings are the actual light values in the current room coming from a light source other than the LED on the NXT Light sensor. Reflective light is measuring the light values returned from the lit LED on the NXT Light Sensor.

Ambient Light

The Light sensor can be used to measure the ambient light in an area by turning off the "Generate light" option on the NXT-G Light Block in your program.. Leaving that option off will allow the sensor to use the light in the room as the main source for the Light sensor. For example, you may have a program that wants to know what the actual light levels are in the robot's current location. If the robot is sitting in a room with little or no light, the ambient light level would be very low. If the location is well lit, the ambient light level would be high. Using these kinds of reading is rare in an FLL-type event. During most robotic competitions, the robot is trying to detect markings on the game field and not really concerned about the actual room lighting.

Reflective Light

We will be using the Light sensor is to read the reflected light levels, which is the intensity that is returned from the surface that the LED light reflects. On our Light sensor block, we will want the "Generate light" option enabled. When properly calibrated, the intensity levels will range from 100 to 0, but when you look at the actual uncalibrated values of the Light sensor, you will see that the range is much smaller, more like 70 to 30. The range is smaller because the Light sensor can read a much wider spectrum of colors than our human eye can see. So the calibration process puts the values into a range that we can find useful. Later, in the "Calibrating the Light Sensor" section, I will describe the process for calibrating the Light sensor.

Positioning the Light Sensor

The location of the Light sensor on your robot is very important to how well the robot will respond when doing line following, and a great deal of the location choice it depends on what type of lines you plan on following. If the Light sensor is located close to the pivot point on your robot, as in Figure 5–1, the corrections the robot makes will be very drastic on a sharp curve. When using a differential steering robot, recall that the pivot point is the midway point of the track, and the track is the distance between the two drive wheels. Put the sensor close to this point, and the robot will overshoot a curve more quickly and will be forced to make drastic corrections to get back on track, thus making the robot seem very jerky when traveling a curved path. On the other hand, if the robot will be commonly following straight lines, having the Light sensor close to the pivot point will give a very smooth response.

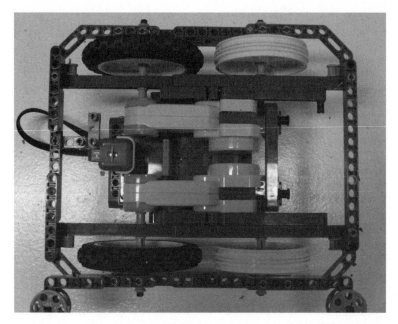

Figure 5–1. DemoBot with a single Light sensor mounted close to the pivot point

Of course, the opposite is true for sensors mounted far ahead of the pivot point, as in Figure 5–2. This forward location is ideal when following an arc, because the robot can make corrections quickly and will not need to make drastic turns. But when traveling on a straight line, more zigzag motion will be seen because the line detection is more sensitive with the Light sensor ahead of the pivot point.

Figure 5–2. DemoBot with a single Light sensor mounted far in front of the Pivot point

Keep the light sensor position and the consequences of its location in mind when analyzing the game field and putting together your strategy for completing the missions. Test frequently and feel free to move the sensor around on your chassis to find what location works best for your design. Do remember that your sensor may need to be recalibrated after each change since its location can have an effect on the light readings.

Calibrating the Light Sensor

One of the things you learn quickly with using light as an input source is that it varies from place to place. The light in your classroom or basement can be very different than the light where the robotics event is being held. The idea behind calibration is to adjust your sensor to the conditions expected in the room.

Depending on the room, you may only need to calibrate one time in the room in which you will be running your robot, even if you are running it multiple times within the same day. But if the room has light conditions that may change, such as large windows that allow in natural sunlight, you need to think about how that light will be changing throughout the day. You may want to calibrate your NXT Light sensors before every run. Proper shielding of your light sensors is important for getting consistent light sensor readings as well; we will talk more about that in later sections.

Don't start calibrating your sensor until you have them located where you want them on your robot's chassis, because changing its location on the chassis can affect the values read by the sensor. Ideally, you're going to want to keep your NXT Light sensor close to the game field; 2–3 centimeters is a safe distance, but makes sure your robot can clear any obstacles that it may have to climb. You don't want your robot getting caught on the sensor because of low ground clearance. I've even seen robots that raise light sensors when more clearance was needed and then lower the sensors when a light reading is needed. Such design is maybe is a bit of over-engineering for an FLL robot, but they are fun to watch.

Making the Calibration

Now, we need to calibrate our sensor so that we can set the real-world values for light and dark. In an ideal environment, the NXT believes white to be maximum light value returned and black to be the minimum value return. These values are represented in the NXT-G code as values between 0 and 100 but rarely will an uncalibrated sensor return either of these two endpoint values. Most of the time, the real values will come back within a range of 30–70.

By calibrating the NXT sensor, we are resetting the limits of the light reading range based on light readings in the current environment. Also, calibrating the light sensor allows the robot to run in different environments without having to actually change the program code to recognize the new room light values.

■ **Note** One year an FLL qualifier was held in an airplane hanger. The location was great, but the lighting was horrible for robots, because every game table in the room had different lighting contrast. This was an excellent opportunity to have a robot that would calibrate its light on each run, and it was too bad our team didn't have such a calibration plan at the time. We did get lucky with a very good run on a table with some consistent lighting; our other runs of the day were not as impressive.

We can perform the calibration in two ways: using NXT-G's own Calibration block that stores the calibrated values in the NXT's memory or by creating our own calibration program that will store the values locally in a file on the NXT brick.

Using the NXT-G Calibration Block

In the NXT-G Advanced tool menu, there is a Calibration block, which is used to calibrate the maximum and minimum levels for both the NXT Light and Sound sensors. The values read by the Calibration block are stored on the NXT brick and remain there until they are deleted or the sensors are recalibrated, even if the NXT brick has been turned off.

■ **Note** If you are using two NXT Light sensors on your robot, the calibration values stored by the Calibration block will be applied to both sensors; the NXT brick does not store separate values for each sensor.

To use the Calibration block, you simply add it to your NXT-G program. Most likely, you would add it in either a separate calibration program or at the beginning of the program you are about to run. If you wish to include calibration in all of your programs and calibrate before each run, creating a My Block with your calibration code would be a good idea.

For example, you could create a My Calibration block; within this block, you would include two Calibration blocks, one to read the minimum light value and one to read the maximum light value. Between the two Calibration blocks, you would write a trigger event such as a Wait block. In the example presented in Figure 5–3, the first Calibration block will read the maximum light value and then wait for the NXT orange button to be pressed before it reads the minimum light value.

The logic for the program shown in Figure 5–3 is as follows:

1. Hold the robot's light sensor over a light area of the field (on a white or very light color), as shown in the left-hand side of Figure 5–4.

2. Press the orange button on the top of the NXT brick.

3. Hear the confirmation tone.

4. Move the robot's light sensor to a dark area of the field (the darker the better), as shown in the right-hand side of Figure 5–4.

5. Press the orange button on the top of the NXT brick.

6. Hear a confirmation tone.

Now, you might want to elaborate on the program. For example, you could add some display prompts to let the user know where to placing the robot's Light sensor and what to do next.

Figure 5–3. *A simple NXT-G calibration program*

Also, if you attach your NXT brick to your computer via the USB cable or Bluetooth and then select Calibrate Sensors from the Tools menu in the NXT programming software, you will be prompted with a dialog box that will allow you to download an NXT-G calibration program to your NXT. That program will work very similar to the one I've just described and will already have all the prompts in place for easy use.

Figure 5–4. *Calibrating theDemoBot light sensor over a light area then over a black line*

Using a Local File

For various reasons, you may not wish to use the Calibration block that comes with NXT-G. For example, perhaps your robot has two light sensors, and you wish to store a separate calibration value for each sensor. The solution is to calibrate from values that you store in a file. You can apply separate calibration values to each sensor by creating your own calibration program and then storing the resulting values in a text file on the NXT brick. You will be able to read that file each time your other programs are run and retrieve the stored light calibration values.

The processing of storing and retrieving from a local file is really not as complicated as it sounds and can be made into really nice program with not too much effort or code. In Figure 5–5, you can see that, instead of using the Calibration block, the code invokes a Light sensor block that copies a value from the Intensity value of the Light Block into a text file. If you are using multiple Light sensors, you could do this same process for each sensor thus allowing you to have a unique light range for each (again, when using the NXT-G Calibration block, the value calibrated is applied to all Light sensors connected to the NXT brick).

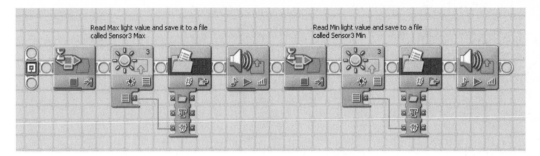

Figure 5-5. An NXT-G calibration program that writes the maximum and minimum values to a text file

To use the values that you saved, your line-following program first reads the saved values from the files and then calculates the desired light value range. That calculation requires a bit more math for a conditional line-following program but fits right into the proportional line follower that I discuss later, in the section on "Line Following."

Viewing the Calibration

One thing that has confuses people about calibration is the process of seeing the newly calibrated values. The NXT brick has a built-in utility to allow you to view the values of its various sensors, but it always displays the uncalibrated values from the Light sensor. So if you use the Calibration block and store new calibration values for the NXT Light sensor in the NXT brick's memory and then use the built-in light sensor viewer, you'll find that it will not show you the newly calibrated values, because it continues to display the original uncalibrated values.

To see the real values, we can write our own Light sensor value viewer that will show us the calibrated values being returned from our light sensor. It's important to know these values so that when we start writing our line-following routines, we know the proper range values our robot will be attempting to detect.

The program is simple, as shown in Figure 5-6. We create a loop that contains a Light Sensor block and is wired to a Number to Text block. The loop will convert the numeric value returned from our Light sensor to text so that we can display it on our NXT screen. The converted value is now passed to the Display block. Then, we wait a second and take another reading of the light sensor.

A program like the one shown in Figure 5-6 will be very helpful in figuring out the initial range for your line-following program, when you're debugging your program, and when you're simply experimenting with different Light sensor positions on your robot chassis. For example, you can move the Light sensor around and get a feel for the difference in light readings based on things such as distance from the game field or even various light sources in your room.

I find it helpful to have such a viewing program running and then shine various light sources at my robot as it sits still on the game field to see what kind of lights have an effect on the reading. Try the lights at various angles too, because many times shadows cause more issues that the light itself.

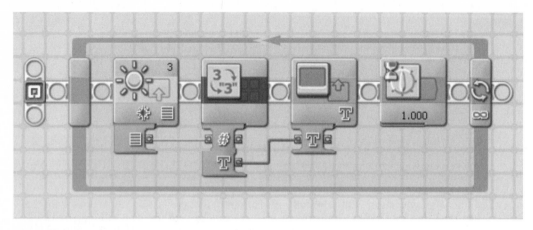

Figure 5–6. A calibrated light value viewer to display calibrated Light sensor values on the NXT screen.

Deleting Calibration Data

The NXT-G Calibration block also has a delete function that will clear out any calibrations currently stored in the NXT brick's memory. It could be helpful to clear out such values at the beginning of your calibration process just so you know you're working with clean values in your NXT brick, especially if you're in a classroom where different people are sharing an NXT brick.

Figure 5–7 shows a basic Calibration deletion program. First, the program waits for the user to press the orange NXT button and then it deletes the current calibration via the Calibration block. Finally, it plays a confirmation tone.

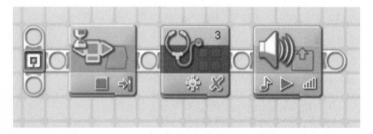

Figure 5–7. A program to delete the current Light sensor calibration

Shielding the Light Sensor

Although calibration of your light sensors is important, shielding the light sensors is just as important if not more. The NXT Light sensor produces its own source of light via the LED, so outside light is really just a nuisance. Many robots that depend on light sensors for navigation work best in a dark room, where the only reflected light they are reading is from the LED on the sensor.

I had one coach tell me that his team's robot had perfect light sensor programming, because it worked just as well with the lights turned off. I hated to tell him that the true test is not removing light sources but adding them. And it's not so much the extra light that will get you as the shadows cast by the lights.

One year, I held a scrimmage match at my home for a few teams, and we quickly realized that my basement wasn't going to be big enough to hold the game tables and the teams, so we moved everything outdoors onto the driveway—in the direct sun light! The shadows cast by the sun as it went behind the trees caused the robots to completely lose control. They were constantly reading shadows as black lines and missing their marks, causing them to make some spectacular crashes on the game field. That scrimmage turned out to be more helpful that we expected, since it showed everyone how sensitive their robots were to the extra lighting. After that day, the teams learned to better shield their light sensors from outside light sources.

The first thing to do is keep the light sensor low and perpendicular to the game field; having the sensor at an angle will not give you the results you desire. Around 3 centimeters off the game field is a good distance. Don't get so close that the sensor can't detect the light, but at the same time, don't get so far away that outside sources have an effect on your readings.

If you can build some kind of cover for your light sensors, this is great for preventing distribution from outside light as well. Many teams will mount the sensors under the bulk of the robot chassis to use the actual robot frame itself to block out the room light. Figure 5–8 shows a robot built with shielding around the light sensors.

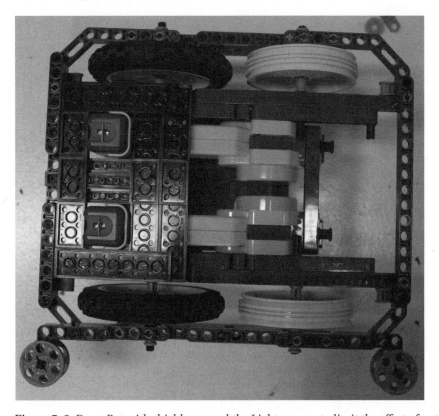

Figure 5–8. DemoBot with shields around the Light sensors to limit the effect of outside light on the light readings

Line Following

In Chapter 3, we talked about going straight and having a well-tuned robot. I mentioned using the field environment for help in traveling a straight line, such as running along the wall of the field with wall followers. Well, another great way to navigate along the field is to follow any lines that may be present on the field map. For example, the FLL 2009 Smart Move field was a line follower's dream. There were nice thick black lines that could guide a robot to most of the important places on the field. In fact, those lines were placed specifically to encourage teams to incorporate line following, or at least line detection, in their robot's logic.

I believe a lot of teams recognize that line following is useful but struggle with how to build and develop a good line-following robot. The code doesn't have to be scary. Yes, you can have some very complicated line-following logic and use lots of fancy algorithms to keep your robot traveling smoothly, but there are simple solutions as well. I will try to explain some of the different techniques available. Remember, though, that these are just examples. I encourage your team to use these as a starting point and build on them; see how much better you can make them.

A Dual-State Example

The simplest of line following programs will be a dual-state program, where the light sensor either sees black or white and adjusts accordingly. The robot is not actually trying to follow the line but is trying to find the edge of it. You just need to decide if you wish to follow the left or the right edge of the line. The robot will oscillate back and forth over the line constantly checking for either black or white values; even if the line is straight, the robot will continue to move back and forth searching for the line. The robot is basically looking for two conditions: a light value that is dark or bright. Based on these values, the robot will either go to the right or the left. In other words, the robot is really working in a mode where it has only two conditions (dark or bright) and two actions (turn left or turn right).

This kind of program is a good start for teams just learning about line following and trying to get a grasp on what is going on with the robot and the code. Most advanced teams will use something a bit more complex or at least smoother running. The more the robot oscillates, the slower it will perform. The goal is to follow the line as straight and as fast as possible.

The code for such logic is fairly simple, as shown in Figure 5–9. We're going to assume that our robot is only using one NXT Light sensor at this point. This example will have a master loop that runs continuously. In a real-world situation, you would need to include some kind of condition that would break the robot out of this loop, but for this example, having the robot stay in a constant line following mode is fine.

We will have a Switch block that uses a Control type of sensor, and the Sensor will be our Light sensor. You will need to also configure what port the Light sensor is connected to on your robot; on DemoBot, the light sensor is connected to port 3.

We are going to assume that the robot's light sensor has been calibrated at this point, so our Compare value for the Switch block is going to use 50 as the middle point. If the light value returned is less than 50 (dark), we will turn the robot to the left looking for a value is greater than 50 (light). You can see that the power settings on the various Motor blocks differ depending on what direction we wish to turn, as we talked about in Chapter 4. Next, we'll loop back and check the Light sensor value again. Again, there is no condition in this loop that will allow our robot to go straight; it will always be going to the left or the right.

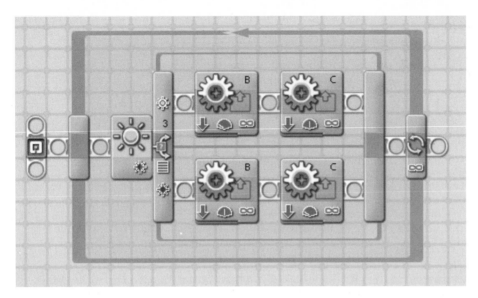

Figure 5–9. A simple line-following program that zig zags back and forth over the line

You will notice that this program is not following the line itself so much as the left edge of the line. If your line has lots of arcs to the right, you might want to switch up the program and follow the right edge of the line instead, since any sudden changes in the direction of the line could cause this simple program to miss the line and send your robot out to Neverland. This type of program works best with lines that stay relatively straight or only curve slightly.

Defining More Than Two States

In the dual-state example, the program only had two conditions to deal with: a light value either greater or less than 50. The problem with that approach is that the robot will tend to overcompensate for changes in the light value. Think of a car traveling down the road and one tire starts to go off the roadway. Turning the car's steering wheel drastically to the left will bring the car back onto the road but could very well cause the car to lose control and run off the other side of the road. Instead, the driver will gradually turn the car back toward the road and remain in control of the car, since the compensative reaction is in relation to the amount of error that needed to be corrected. We can do the same thing with our LEGO robots by adding more conditions to our switch logic.

Think about the value returned from a calibrated light sensor; it will be between 0 and 100. If the value is close to 0, we are going to want to make a more drastic change in our direction compared to a value around 35, where we'd need only a slight correction in direction. What we do is divide our possible light range (0–100) into smaller sections. Let's create a series of five smaller ranges (numbered 0–4) by dividing 100 by 20; this will give us new condition values that we will use in our Switch block. I refer to this method as the *complex condition* method. Table 5–1 shows what code we will put for each condition in our code.

Table 5–1. *Complex State Conditions*

Range Value	Action
0	Turn sharply to the left; slow down motor B.
1	Turn slightly to the left; slow down motor B slightly.
2	Stay straight; keep both motors equal.
3	Turn slightly to the right; slow down motor C slightly.
4	Turn sharply to the right; slow down motor C.

Our example code, shown in Figure 5–10, will again contain a master loop that runs continuously with a Light sensor block. The Intensity value from the Light sensor block will be wired to a Math block, where we will divide the intensity value by 20 and round it off to the closest value. This value will be what we pass to the Switch block. Since it is possible to get a return value of 5 when the light value is higher than 90, we simply just set our condition 4 as the default condition on our Switch block, thus forcing condition 5 to implement the same actions as condition 4.

Within each condition of the Switch block, the Move blocks are set at various power levels to force the robot to turn in one direction or the other, but when the condition value is 2, both Motor blocks are set to the same power level to allow the robot to travel straight.

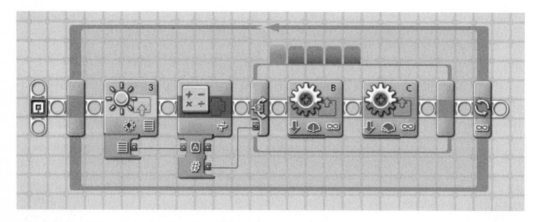

Figure 5–10. *A complex condition line-following program with five conditions in the Switch block*

Implementing a Proportional Algorithm

If you want to make line following, especially of curved lines, even smoother, you could take the complex state method and break down the light sensor Intensity value even more. For example, you could go from five conditional states to ten. Eventually though, you'll have more conditions that you'll want to manage in NXT-G; large Switch blocks can become very clumsy to deal with them in the NXT-G interface. One solution is to implement a proportional algorithm.

Whenever you start talking to anyone about robotics and line following, the term "PID" will come up; it stands for *proportional, integral, and derivative.* But most LEGO NXT-G programs that people claim are PID really are just "P." For NXT-G, a proportional type of program is very doable, while a full PID program is a bit much to for such a simple programming language (but I'm sure someone, somewhere, has implemented the PID approach in NXT-G).

A proportional system uses a bit of math to calculate the amount of correction that is needed to get the robot back on the line that it is following. Instead of using a set value to correct the direction of the robot, we actually calculate the direction change based on the value read by the light sensor. If the error value is small, the robot corrects very slightly, whereas a larger value results in a stronger correction.

We'll begin our example of a proportional NXT-G by creating the Variable blocks described in Table 5–2.

Table 5–2. Variable Definitions Used in the Proportional Line Following Program

Variable	Description
MidRange	This value will be the middle value between our minimum and maximum light readings. If the light sensor is calibrated with a minimum value of 0 and maximum of 100, the MidRange will be 50.
Gain	The Gain variable will be used to fine-tune our error correction. If the robot is zigzagging too much, set Gain to a value less than 1. If the robot is not responding fast enough, set Gain a bit higher to adjust the correction.
Power	This is the power that the robot will travel at when going straight, and this value should be adjusted between 30 and 70, depending on your robot's design. Be careful not to set the value too high, or the robot might miss the line.
Error	The Error value is calculated by our MidRange variable from the Intensity light value, and it will be used when we set the correction to the robot's motors.
Correction	Correction will be our Gain applied to the Error amount. This will give us the difference need that we apply to the Power variable that is then applied to the motors.

Now, the logic in our code is fairly simple, as shown in Figure 5–11. We first calculate our Error value by subtracting the MidRange value from the Intensity value returned from the Light sensor. Next, we calculate the Correction value by multiplying the calculated Error by Gain. The Correction value will be applied to our Power value and then passed to the Motor block. The trick is to invert the value between the two motors, so for Motor block B, we will add the Correction to the Power, and for Motor block C, we will subtract the Correction from the Power. You can see in Figure 5–11 this logic put into a NXT-G program. Remember that different robot designs will require some adjustments to the Power, Gain, and MidRange depending on your robot's response.

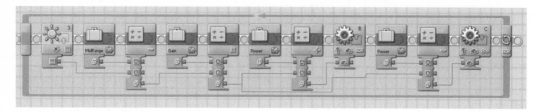

Figure 5–11. *The proportional line-following program does not use a Switch block and instead calculates the nessary power to drive the motors and keep the robot on the line.*

Using Dual Light Sensors

The examples so far have all dealt with robots using a single light sensor to detect the edge of the line you were following. But what if you added a second light sensor and straddled the line? The FLL rules do allow for two Light sensors, even though none of the LEGO MINDSTORMS kits include a second sensor (you can purchase a second sensor separately if desired).

When you have two Light sensors, you are going to want them to be spaced on your robot just a bit wider than the line you will be trying to follow. Set them too close together and you'll never get a valid state for going straight; too far apart and you will find your robot over compensating for direction changes when it hits the line. Ideally, neither sensor will see the line when the robot is centered over the line; they should only see the area next to the line. In Figure 5–13, you can see the DemoBot with two light sensors installed.

If we wanted to use the complex state method we talked about previously, we simply add a second Switch block, so there's one for each Light sensor, and each Switch block would now only have three conditions as shown in Table 5–3.

Table 5–3. *Complex State Conditions for Robots with Dual Light Sensors*

Light Sensor	Range Value	Action
Left	0	Turn sharply to the left; slow down motor B.
Left	1	Turn slightly to the left; slow down motor B slightly.
Right and Left	2	Stay straight; keep both motors equal.
Right	1	Turn slightly to the right; slow down motor C slightly.
Right	0	Turn sharply to the right, slow down motor C.

Both Light sensors need to start off straddling the line. If the robot gets into a position in which both light sensors see black, the robot will simply slow down. That's because the conditional switches would slow down both motors, and thus try to force the robot to turn in both directions at once. This can happen when a robot leaves base expecting a line to follow just outside of base and it detects the border around the base. To remedy this, either a delay needs to be added to the program when leaving base to prevent line detection, or you just allow the robot to slow down when it first detects the border then speed up again after it is past the border. Figure 5–12 shows and example of how you could write dual Light sensor logic in NXT-G.

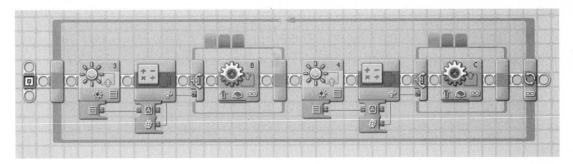

Figure 5–12. *A complex condition line-following program for dual Light sensors, with a Switch block for each Light sensor and only three conditions*

Figure 5–13. *DemoBot with dual Light sensors installed*

Line Detection

The lines on a game field can serve other uses for navigation besides line following. Various areas on a game field often are outlined by a line of some sort. The outline might not even be a true line, just a shape or an image of some sort. These graphics are still important and can be very helpful when trying to determine if a robot is in the right location. Also, be aware that these lines might not simple black lines; many times, they will be colored lines and requite a bit more effort to detect properly with a NXT Light sensor.

In the game field for FLL 2008 Climate Connections (see Figure 5–14), parts of the field were outlined with various colored lines. These were very useful when trying to navigate to a given area to perform a task. What made them tricky to use was the fact that they were colored lines. Also, you had to cross over a large rainbow printed on the mat. The solution wasn't as simple as driving forward until encountering, say, a red line. You had to time when your robot would begin looking at the correct red line and move past the rainbow, or you had to count how many red lines you encountered.

Let's talk about finding lines in general. Then we'll look at how color lines appear to an NXT Light sensor.

Finding a Line

If you take a look at the 2008 FLL Climate Connections field mat shown in Figure 5–14, you will see that it doesn't have a lot of lines that would be helpful for line following. However, there are lots of thick lines that either outline or could guide a robot to a particular location on the field. These lines aren't there just for looking pretty. They are there for you to use to help your robot navigate to particular locations. In the middle of the field, you will see a lot of open space, and it would be very easy for your robot to get lost in this space. Having the borders enables you to better program your robot to detect when it has reached a location that you are targeting.

Say, for example, your robot leaves base and is heading to the location I've marked as "Zone A". After the robot leaves base, it will be very dependent on odometry to find its way across the field. During this time, it should start looking for the thick black border around Zone A using its Light sensor. You will have to be careful that the other colors on the field don't confuse your robot. In real life, that rainbow at the bottom of Figure 5–14 tripped up many robots. You need to think, when planning the task for your missions, about what things can be in your way. What other markings on the mat can confuse your robot?

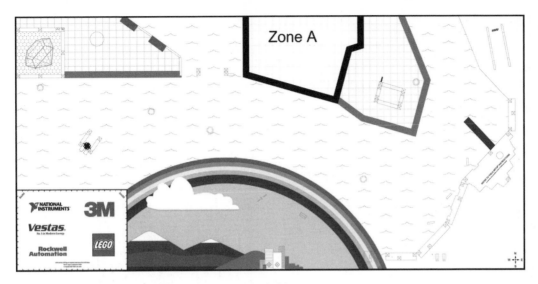

Figure 5–14. The 2008 FLL Climate Connections field mat

Now, look at the FLL 2007 Power Puzzle field mat in Figure 5–15; it was very different from the 2008 Climate Connections mat in that it had much better defined zones with easy-to-track borders. There were a few roads that you could use for line following. Plus, the blue rivers were great for breaking up the different areas of the mat, giving your robot quick feedback for where it was located currently on the field. Notice the three obvious black lines down the middle of the mat crossing the robot's path as it leaves base heading north. Counting these lines is a great way to help the robot learn where it is located.

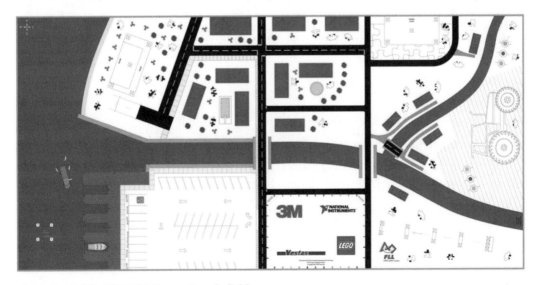

Figure 5–15. The 2007 FLL Power Puzzle field mat

Now, when you count lines, remember that you cannot just count how many times your light sensor sees a black line, because as a light sensor travels over a line, it will read it multiple times. You will have to include edge-detection logic in your code, along the following lines:

1. Look for a black line, or rather a black reading.

2. Increment a counter when black is encountered.

3. Begin looking for a transition to white, (i.e., for a white reading).

4. Go back to step 1 when white is encountered.

Once you find white, start looking for black again; this process would continue for however many lines you're expecting to encounter. In Figure 5–16, you can see an example of what such code would look like in NXT-G.

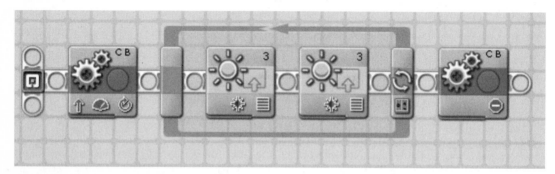

Figure 5–16. An NXT-G line-counter program

In this NXT-G line-counter code, the robot runs forward and waits for the Light sensor block to detect a black line. Then, the next Light sensor block will wait to find the next nonwhite area, letting us know that we have completely crossed the black line. When the loop counter reaches three, this Loop block exit and the Move block at the end will stop the robot.

Detecting Color in Lines

You will notice that, on the field mats in Figures 5–14 and 5–15, many of the lines or areas are not simple black-and-white lines; actually, many of them are colored lines or edges. Even though we're using the NXT Light sensor and not the NXT Color sensor, we can still detect different colors. We do so by interpreting the different colors as shades of grey. The values returned for a given color will fall somewhere in the spectrum between 0 for white and 100 for black.

Ideally, you will still be able to calibrate your Light sensor on a white-and-black source, and the color values will fall between the calibrated range of 0–100. It is best to first calibrate your Light sensor, and then by using the light value view program place your light sensor over the various colors on the game field map and use the light value view program to read and record the values for each color. As long as you can calibrate your robot consistently the color values should be read the same.

Be careful! Some colors will share the same value. For example, many times red, green, and gray will return the same intensity values to the NXT Light sensor. This is why it is important to get a good reading on each color and keep track of which values register the most consistent results.

Also, when you are thinking through your strategies for navigating a game field, look for colors that contrast more drastically with other colors to help avoid confusion and make finding the navigation points easier. Thick lines are, of course, going to make better markers than thin or fussy lines and edges. You are really looking for anything unique that can produce consistent readings back to your program. Consistent markings are going to produce consistent results.

Summary

Light Sensors are one of the most helpful sensors when trying to navigate most robotics game fields. In FLL the game field maps are full of clues that can be utilized by Light Sensors. Many teams will shy away from using them just because they have a bit of a learning curve when first using them. But almost all winning teams take advantage of Light Sensors when navigating the field....

CHAPTER 6

■ ■ ■

Squaring Up

After learning about going straight and turning, you're now able to give your robot just enough information to get seriously lost on the game field. No matter how well your robot navigates in any direction, it won't take long before it loses track of where it is facing. This is just the nature of LEGO robots; they're never going to be consistently accurate without a little help and some realignment.

When your robot starts running a few missions, you'll notice that after just a few navigation changes, such as going straight, turning 90 degrees, going straight again, and then maybe backing up, it will rarely end up in the exact same place again, much less be pointing in the same direction each time. When you plan your robot's missions, it's always a good idea to build in some expectations of error by about an inch. Doing so will be important when you're thinking through your strategies for completing a mission. But there also ways to use your environment to get your robot pointing in the right direction even after you've left base.

Winning robots will constantly realign themselves throughout the game to ensure consistency for each mission they attempt. The trick is to locate the points on the game field that your robot can align with to get the best results. You're looking for anything that is a constant on the field, things that don't move and remain in the same position relative to the rest of the field at all times. Such things can be markers printed on the game field, such as lines or shapes or the actual walls of the game table itself, which can be very useful when the game mat is lined up properly on the table. Or there could be actual field objects that are affixed to the mat throughout the game and won't be moving or removed.

When you are coming up with your mission strategies, think about things that can help you square up your robot again after just a few moves. Is there a wall close by after you make a 90-degree turn? What about the field mat; is there some kind of line or border that your robot can try to detect and line up with? Maybe the mission object itself has some way for you to use it to square up before or after you've completed the mission. These are all things you want to think about as you do your planning. They will be the keys to having successful and accurate robot runs.

Squaring Up with Walls

One of the obvious objects to use for aligning your robot is a wall of the game table. Most LEGO robot events will have either walls or field edges that you can use to square up with. In FLL, every game has them; every season they are one of the true constants of FLL games. This is one reason that it is important to have a game table when practicing for an FLL event. I know some schools don't have room for the tables in their classrooms, so teams just lay the field mats on the classroom floor during meetings. While this works well for space conservation in the classroom, it will not prepare your team for the actual game-day competition environment. To be successful in winning an FLL event, you are going to need a practice field that's as close as possible to what you'll be running on at your robot event.

You have already learned that the table walls are our friends because we can use them to help us go straight in wall following, and now you know that they can help us get our robot back on track and facing the right direction. There are multiple ways to line up a robot using the walls: we can include sensors on our robots to detect the walls or use some simple passive techniques.

Passive Wall Squaring

Let's say your robot has traveled straight, parallel to the table wall, down the game field and made a 90-degree turn. Afterward, you would expect the rear of your robot to be perpendicular to the wall of the table, and if you built a proper robot and followed some of the techniques we talked about in previous chapters, most likely you would correct. But what if there was a ripple in the mat or one of your wheels slipped some when you turned? A number of things could mess up your robot's navigation. How do you guarantee that your robot is pointing in the correct direction?

The easy way would be to simply back up the robot into the wall. If your robot has a nice flat, even back surface, you can simply slowly back up the robot until it meets the wall and then push against the wall until your robot chassis is flush with the wall. This is a passive method because we're not using any kind of sensors to detect the wall; we're simply using some time and pushing up to the wall until we assume we're straight with it. You can see in Figure 6–1 that DemoBot's rear chassis is designed to allow for flush contact with the wall.

Figure 6–1. DemoBot has a flat rear surface on the chassis to allow for flush contact with the wall when squaring up.

The passive approach only works if your robot chassis is flat on the back. If anything extends beyond the back of the robot, that extension will contact the wall and could cause the robot to wind up in an undesired angle for your next approach. So again, for this approach to work, you need a rear surface or even bumper on the your robot's chassis that is square with your robot's drive system and will allow the robot to become square when pushed flush with a flat surface, such as the table walls. Also, be sure that the contact point on your robot is fairly centered in height relative to your robot's chassis as well. If it is too low or high, you could get unexpected results as the robot pushes against the wall. The goal is to make a nice smooth touch and gently line up the robot. You can see in Figure 6–2 that the robot fails to square up properly, because access to the rear of the robot's chassis is obstructed, but in Figure 6–3, DemoBot has no problem squaring up with the wall.

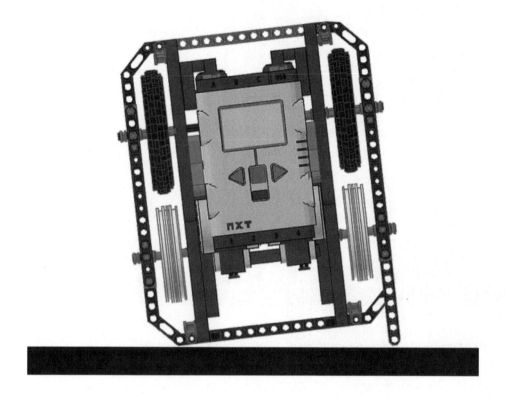

Figure 6–2. Something extending beyond the robot chassis can prevent a flush match with the wall.

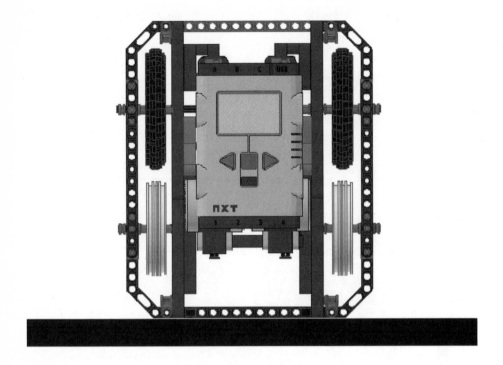

Figure 6–3. A smooth rear chassis allows for the robot to square up flush with the wall.

Code for implementing the passive approach is very simple; a Move block with both drive motors running at the same slow, steady speed toward the walls is all that is needed. Since we are not using any kind of sensors to detect the wall itself, a duration of time can be set for executing the Move block. The actual time used will have to be calculated based on how far the robot is expected to be from the wall at the time. It's a safe bet to give the robot an extra second or two to help a robot that is further off angle than expected. In Figure 6–4, you can see a sample program that aligns the robot with the wall after making a 90-degree turn, and Figure 6–5 shows the path the robot took when running the sample program.

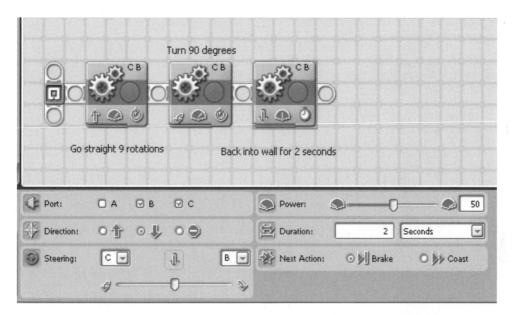

Figure 6–4. The Move block at the end of the program will allow our robot to square up with the wall, giving it 2 seconds to do so.

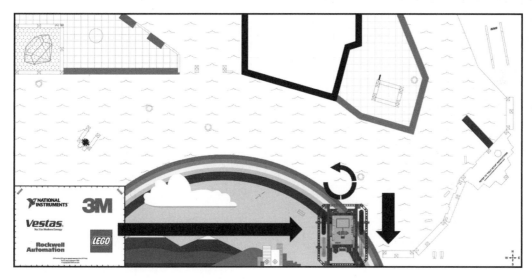

Figure 6–5. The path that the robot follows as it follows the code in Figure 6–4: After making the 90-degree turn, the robot backs up and squares with the wall.

I would avoid using rotation or degrees for your duration, because doing so can cause the robot to get stuck. With passive wall squaring, we're expecting some tire slippage when the robot makes contact with the wall, but if this slippage doesn't occur and we're using rotation or degrees as the duration, the duration value will never be met since the tires are not slipping, thus causing the robot to become stuck. With time as the duration, even if the robot does not spin the tires, the duration value will be met, since time is not dependent on tire spin.

Interactive Wall Squaring

If you desire a little more feed back when aligning your robot with the wall or other field object, Touch Sensors on the rear of your robot can come in handy. The most straight-forward system would be to mount two NXT Touch Sensors on the rear corners of your robot chassis. You will want to keep them spaced at a distance close to the width of your robot to help ensure that the robot is truly lined up square with the wall.

The advantage of receiving feedback when touching the walls is that you remove the guesswork we had with a passive solution. Instead of our program relying on duration of time, it will simply have the robot back up till both touch sensors have triggered a positive response, letting the program know that the robot is aligned and ready for the next statement in the program.

The disadvantages of such an alignment method are that you have used up two sensor ports on your NXT brick and two NXT Touch Sensors. Now, if you can make use of these sensors this configuration for some of your other mission task, using them for squaring up is not a disadvantage at all. For example, you may use the sensors for alignment but also use them to detect when your robot reached a mission object. In Chapter 7, we'll talk about bumpers and Touch Sensors for helping detect such objects.

In Figure 6–6, you can see DemoBot configured with a pair of NXT Touch Sensors on its rear chassis. As the robot backs into the wall for alignment, the Touch Sensors may trigger at separate times depending on the approach angle of the robot. The NXT-G brick will be programmed to continue driving backward slowly until the Pressed condition state of each Touch Sensors is met, as shown in the sample program Figure 6–7.

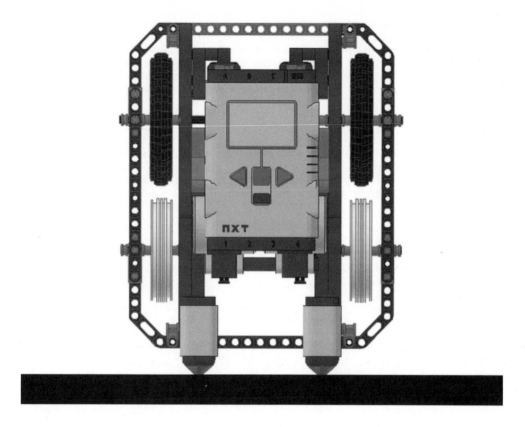

Figure 6–6. DemoBot with dual NXT Touch Sensors installed on the rear of the chassis for interactive wall detection

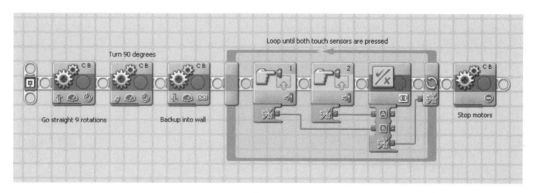

Figure 6–7. An NXT-G program driving the robot into reverse into the wall until both NXT Touch Sensors have been pressed

When using NXT Touch Sensors for alignment, it is very important to put the touch sensors in a location on the robot from which they will make solid contact with the wall or object that you are attempting to detect. One year when judging at the FLL World Festival, I witnessed a team using such a technique for alignment, but it had put the robot's sensors too low. The robot chassis actually flexed some when the robot made contact, preventing one of the two Touch Sensors from ever completely pressing in far enough to detect the wall. This caused the robot to get stuck where it was as it continued to try to drive in reverse while waiting for both sensors to detect the wall.

The sad scenario I've just described could have been avoided in two ways. First, the team could have raised the sensor higher on the robot to move it closer to the actual robot chassis, so the chassis didn't flex as much when making impact. Even some extra bracing would have helped. Second, the team could have added some logic to the robot that said, "Move backward until both Touch Sensors are pressed or until 3 seconds have passed." Adding that second duration condition of time would require a bit fancier programming, but it would have saved the team in competition. In your own designs though, you may prefer to focus on the simplicity of good structural design as a way of avoiding the problem.

■ **Tip** You can implement a similar approach using two NXT Light Sensors located on the rear of your robot chassis facing up toward the wall instead of down at the game mat, and just look for both sensors to be in a state where they no longer read ambient light from the room. However, this approach is not likely going to be the best use of your light sensors. If you really desire feedback when aligning with the wall, use the NXT Touch Sensors. They are better designed for such usage.

Aligning with Lines and Edges

Besides the table walls, most game fields will have some type of printing or markings on the field that your robot can use for alignment. You can align with those markings with light sensors, using some of the techniques discussed earlier in Chapter 5. The trick is that you need to use a second NXT Light Sensor for alignment. Only one is included in the LEGO MINDSTORMS kits, but a second one can be purchased for a relatively small cost.

Aligning the robot using field markings can be very effective and can give you a bit more flexibility than solely relying on the table walls. Of course, ideally, your robot will take advantage of both types of squaring—wall and field marking. With the field markings, you will be able to align the robot with various angles depending on the actual markings on the field. For example, in Figure 6–5, which shows the FLL 2008 Climate Connections game field, you can see that different areas have nice thick colored lines outlining them. These lines, if used correctly, where great for helping line up a robot for some of the various missions.

We will use the line as we did the walls for lining up, but instead of being pushing up to the wall, we will need to have some smart code for our NXT to recognize that we are at the line and to determine which direction the robot will need to turn to align itself with the line or marking.

First, we will mount two NXT Light Sensors to the robot and make sure they are parallel with each other and as wide apart as we can get them on our chassis. Having the sensors far part allows our robot to make less-drastic turns when lining up . The closer together the sensors are located, the faster the second sensor will approach the line edge as the robot turns to square up to the line. A greater distance between sensors will allow for a smooth and precise alignment. If this doesn't make sense right now, don't worry; it will once we talk more about the logic involved to turn the robot.

Begin the alignment process by turning on both Light Sensors and searching for the color line that you have been told to expect. For example, say the mission we're going to tackle has a black line in front of it. Well, you know from Chapter 5 that a black line will register a low number reading on our Light Sensor. So our NXT-G code, as shown in Figure 6–8, will tell each light sensor to be on the lookout for a light reading with a low number, maybe 30 or lower depending on if there is any other printing on the field that we need to be concerned with reading by accident. We don't want to trigger a false positive on something that is not our line.

Now, let's say that the robot is running along and the Light Sensor on the right side of our robot detects a black line. Now, we need to find the line with the left Light Sensor. All the robot has to do is stop moving forward and turn to the right until the left Light Sensor also detects the line. Once both Light Sensors have found the edge of the line, the robot should now be aligned with that line.

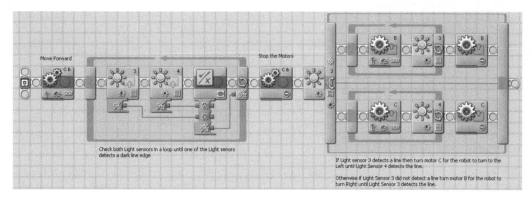

Figure 6–8. NXT-G program aligning the robot with a line detected on the game field using NXT Light sensors

So, what is your robot actually doing? It's using the first Light Sensor that detected the line as a pivot point. Your robot then turns along that pivot point until the other Light Sensor reaches the line, as shown in Figure 6–9. Again, having the light sensors a good distance apart from each other ensures that you get a nice straight alignment with the line. If the sensors are too close together, it leaves much more room for error when making proper alignment.

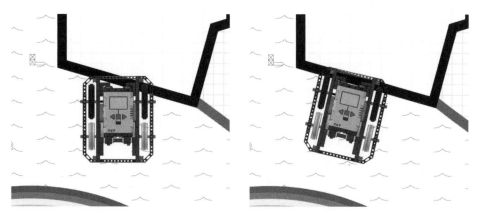

Figure 6–9. DemoBot aligns itself with the black line border using Light Sensors on the front of the robot chassis. The first Light Sensor detects the line, and then the robot pivots until the second Light Sensor detects the line.

Summary

Knowing that the robot is aligned with the edge of a line or wall can be very powerful in accurate navigation. Good alignment gives the robot a sense of where it's facing on the field. If your robot can make such alignments after every few navigation moves, you will have a robot that can move around the game field with confidence, and you won't have to worry about things such as ripples in the mat, extra tire spin, or even an unexpected field object hitting your robot. Winning robots are self-correcting, and the concept of field alignment is a key part of that.

CHAPTER 7

■ ■ ■

Collision Detection

Now that our robot is navigating the field, it can move straight, turn, and even realign itself on a straight course. But what happens when there is something in its way? How does it know when it is about to run into something on the game field? We need to make the robot smart enough to avoid obstacles and navigate past them. Just like a person, the robot needs to take advantage of all its senses and learn how to react properly to obstacles in its path.

LEGO MINDSTORMS sensors give your robot a variety of sensors that you can take advantage of during a robotics event. Some we have already talked about in previous chapters, but here, we will focus on how to use them for collision detection and obstacle avoidance. We have touch sensors to know when the robot comes in contact with something. The ultrasonic sensors can be used to detect when we are close to an object. We can even use the light sensor in some occasions to sense pending collisions or when contact has actually been made.

Touch Sensor

Imagine trying to walk around in a dark room. You can't see anything so you have to rely on your sense of touch; you would feel the walls and any other objects that may be in the room. The robot can do the same thing using the NXT Touch Sensor.

The LEGO MINDSTORM Education NXT kit comes with two NXT Touch Sensors. The Touch Sensor is one of the easiest sensors to use and to include in NXT-G code. The Touch Sensor has three states to detect: pressed, and bumped. Each one of these states can be taken advantage of when using the touch sensor for collision detection.

■ **Note** On the NXT-G Touch Sensor block, the data hub values for the Action wire are 0 for pressed, 1 for released, and 2 for bumped.

Monitoring the Pressed State

Monitoring the pressed state of the touch sensor is the most common way to use the Touch Sensor. Pressed is simply when the Touch Sensor has had its activator pressed into the sensor, as simple as it sounds. The activator doesn't have to be completely pushed for the touch sensor to trigger a positive pressed state to the NXT-G code.

On your robot, the Touch Sensor can be mounted on the front of the robot for simple touch detection when the robot bumps into an obstacle. Once a positive touch is registered, the robot can decide how to react to coming in contact with the object. For example, you may want your robot to run forward until it runs into the far end of the field table and then turn to the left. Figure 7–1 shows the simple NXT-G logic of such an approach, and Figure 7–2 shows the DemoBot with a single NXT Touch Sensor installed on the front of the frame.

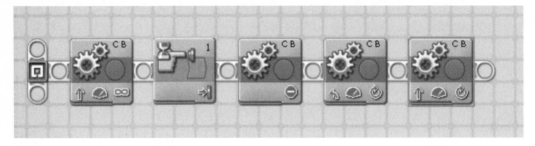

Figure 7–1. *A simple NXT-G program that drives forward until Touch Sensor is pressed and then stops and turns.*

Figure 7–2. *DemoBot with single Touch Sensor installed*

You might notice that with the Touch Sensor simply mounted to the front of the robot frame the area of touch is rather small. It only registers a pressed state when the small space of the Touch Sensor makes contact. The touch area is the area that needs to make contact with the obstacle to register a pressed state. For example, the NXT Touch Sensor itself has a rather small touch area, since the actuator on the front of the sensor is less than an inch in width.

You can give your field of touch a much larger contact area by adding a bumper. A bumper on our robot will be built in such a way that the NXT Touch Sensor isn't making direct contact with the obstacle but indirectly through the bumper's lever. A robot bumper can either be the entire width of the robot frame or maybe just a smaller area depending on your robot strategy.

Figure 7–3 is an example of a single touch bumper that can be attached to the front of a robot that will trigger the Touch Sensor's pressed state when the bumper makes contact with an object. The small rubber belt on the bumper keeps the Touch Sensor in an unpressed state then the bumper is not making contact with an obstacle. You don't want the bumper to trigger a false positive touch result when it hasn't actually bumped into anything.

Figure 7–3. *A single Touch Sensor bumper assembly*

A large single touch bumper on a robot can be problematic depending on the size of the bumper . If it's too wide, the contact with the target will have to be greater so that the lever makes a clean press of the Touch Sensor. Or if the bumper is too flimsy, it can get caught on obstacles as well. Adding a second NXT Touch Sensor can be helpful in increasing the robot's touch sensitivity by dividing the touch area among the two sensors. In Figure 7–4, we have a bumper with two independent NXT Touch Sensors giving the robot a larger touch area.

Figure 7–4. *A double Touch Sensor bumper assembly*

With two Touch Sensors, your code will have to be a bit smarter than with just one sensor, and it will use some Logic blocks to make it aware that one of the sensors was touched. The code in Figure 7–5 shows that the two Touch Sensor blocks feed into the one Logic block using an OR parameter so that if the Touch Sensor in port 1 or port 2 is pressed, the condition as been met for the code to execute the next code block.

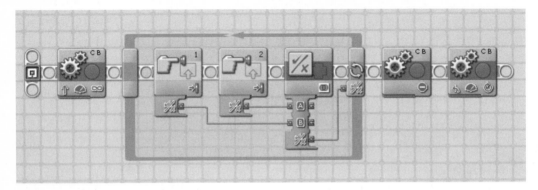

Figure 7–5. NXT-G code testing for either Touch Sensor block to be pressed by inputing the results into a Logic block

Now, depending on your strategy, you may want to know which Touch Sensor was pressed and react differently based on this information. So you would change your NXT-G code to use a Switch block to determine what action to perform after the touch event happens, as shown in Figure 7–6.

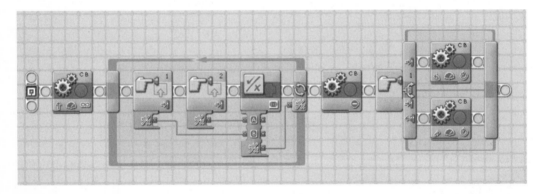

Figure 7–6. NXT-G code that turns in different directions based on which Touch Sensor was pressed

The code in Figure 7–6 will loop until one of the Touch Sensors is pressed. Then the code will stop the robot. Control next flows into the Switch block, which decides whether the robot needs to turn left or right. If the first Touch Sensor is pressed, the robot will go to the left; otherwise, it will go right.

Detecting the Released State

The idea of detecting when a Touch Sensor is pressed is pretty simple, but there are times when it's important to know when the Touch Sensor has been released. The release state is returned from the Touch Sensor whenever the actuator has returned to its normal position after being pressed. In a program, it may be important to know that the robot is no longer making contact with the object that it came in contact with originally. For example, your code could have logic that tells the robot to back up when the Touch Sensor is pressed then back up until the Touch Sensor is released, as shown in Figure 7–7.

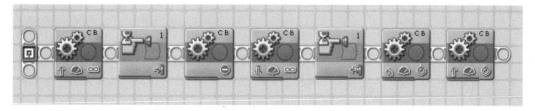

Figure 7–7. *NXT-G code that stops when Touch Sensor one is pressed, backs up until Touch Sensor one is released,and then turns to the left and continues straight*

It could also be that the Touch Sensor starts out in a pressed state and the robot wants to know when an action happens that causes the robot's Touch Sensor to be in a release state. In Figure 7–8, you can see an example of a bumper that is normally in the pressed state, and when contact is made, the bumper will release the sensor. One of the advantages of such a design is that if the bumper makes a hard impact with the obstacle the sensor does not take the actual impact the force is removed from the sensor. The rubber belts are actually acting like shock absorbers and taking the energy of the impact. This can be important when you have a fast moving robot that tends to hit things a bit hard.

Figure 7–8. *A release state bumper that, when pressed, releases the the NXT Touch Sensor instead of pressing it*

Maybe the robot has a claw attachment that carries a box. When the box is placed in its proper location by the robot, the robot's program needs to know when the claw has fully released the box. If the Touch Sensor is in the claw attachment, once the sensor reaches a released state, the robot now knows that the box has been released by the robot. Another example would be if the Touch Sensor is mounted in the robot chassis in such a way that it's facing the opposite direction of the expected touch impact. If you have a clever enough design, you could make it so that when the Touch Sensor reaches a released state that the robot knows it has made contact with an object.

Also the released state can be a good way to find out if your robot is stuck somewhere on the field. For example, say your robot has a bumper on the front of the robot, and you're expecting it to hit a wall and then back up. If the released state of the NXT Touch Sensor is never met after the pressed state, you know something has gone wrong since you expect the bumper to release when the robot moves away from the wall that it touched. If this is the case, your code could try to run some alternative code to get your robot unstuck from its location. Granted, this scenario is not common, but if you know your robot could get into such a situation, it never hurts to have some extra logic in your code to handle it.

Achieving the Bumped State

The bumped state on the NXT Touch Sensor is achieved when the sensor makes a full press and release of the actuator on the sensor with in a time frame of 5 seconds. The bumped state is not very helpful when detecting a collision with the wall or an object. Since the Touch Sensor does not return a value until the full bump is complete, so if a robot needs to change direction when the object or wall is detected, the code won't know of the collision until the Touch Sensor is both pressed and released. But if the robot it working to detect its position on the field by counting the number of obstacles it passes or brushes against, the bump can be helpful.

In the 2009 Smart Moves game, the field had a series of LEGO walls that contained a number of TECHNIC axles pointing upward. By creating a clever attachment using the Touch Sensor and some gears, you can enable your robot to count how many axles it comes into contact with as it passes by the LEGO wall. Then, the logic in the NXT-G could simply keep track of how many times the Touch Sensor reaches a bumped state. Figure 7–9 shows such a sensor.

If we know that, when the robot reaches the fourth axle, it will need to activate a motorized attachment, we can write code to make that happen. The code would look something like the code shown in Figure 7–10.

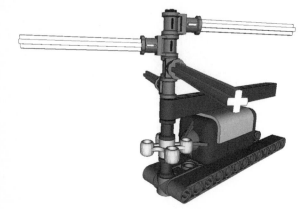

Figure 7–9. A touch counter that registers a bump touch each time the knob gear makes a quarter turn

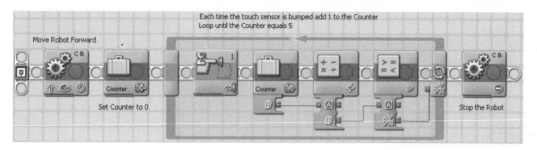

Figure 7–10. In this NXT-G code used by the bump counter attachment, the code counts to 5 and then stops the robot.

Light Sensor

In most situations, the NXT Light Sensor is not one of the better choices for collision detection because of how the sensor works. The sensor looks for levels of light reflected back to the sensor's input device; detecting objects with such a method would be unpredictable at best. Light sensors are great for detecting markings on the game field but not so good at detecting when the robot has come in contact with an obstacle.

In theory, you could have the Light Sensor facing forward, and when it detects no reflected light at all, assume your robot has made contact with a wall or other object, but you couldn't be sure since other things such as shadows or changing light conditions could produce false positive results.

One trick you could use that makes use of the NXT Light Sensor for collision detection would be to build a special bumper that gives the Light Sensor different readings when the bumper is pressed. In Figure 7–11, you can see a Light Sensor mounted over a set of black TECHNIC beams. When the bumper is in its resting state, the sensor would read a low light level since it is pointing at the black beams. But when the bumper is pressed, as in Figure 7–12, the black beams are removed from in front of the Light Sensor and a higher light level reading would be read.

Having a properly calibrated Light Sensor would be important when using a Light Sensor in such a way due to the fact that outside light sources could affect the levels of light that are read by the sensor when the bumper is closed or open.

Figure 7–11. *A Light Sensor being used to detect touch by a bumper that blocks the Light Sensor's path with black beams*

Figure 7–12. *With the bumper pushed the black beams are removed from the view of the Light sensor.*

The NXT-G code for using such a bumper would be very similar to the code used when a Touch Sensor is involved. In the code sample in Figure 7–13, you can see that the robot will move forward for an unlimited amount of time, so long as the light sensor senses back. Once the Light Sensor no longer sees black, the robot will stop and then back up.

Figure 7–13. *NXT-G code using at Light Sensor as a touch detector*

Ultrasonic Sensor

The NXT Ultrasonic Sensor can be very helpful in detecting large object on the game field. The sensor works by sending out a sonic wave and allowing it to reflect off of objects in front of the sensor. The wave reflects back to the sensor, and the sensor determines the distance based on how long it took for the sonic wave to return. The Ultrasonic Sensor should always be mounted in a horizontal position for actuate readings. Using units of centimeters instead of inches works best when trying to detect close objects. Distances less than 3 millimeters cannot be read accurately by the sensor. Also, the accuracy is decreased when objects are further than 25 centimeters from the sensor as well. The optimum range for the Ultrasonic Sensor is between 3 centimeters and 25 centimeters. It can also be noted that the left side of the sensor is the receiver, meaning the sensor is stronger at detecting objects on the right side of the sensor where the sonic signal is transmitted.

With the Ultrasonic Sensor, using the View tools built into the NXT brick are very helpful in calculating the distance of objects and proper placement of the sensor on your robot. Experiment with various locations to see what position gives you the most consistent measurement when trying to detect a particular object on the field.

When using the Ultrasonic Sensor in a competition where other robots are running close by, such as FLL events, it is a good idea to keep the sensor mounted lower than the walls on the game table. There is a possibility that if another robot is also using an Ultrasonic Sensor, that sensor might confuse the sensor on your robot if sonic signals are detected from the other robot. By keeping your sensor lower than the table walls, you will avoid such confusion.

The Ultrasonic Sensor works very well at detecting large flat objects but will not detect smaller or rounded objects accurately. In the 2009 FLL Smart Moves games, there were a series of sensor walls that the robots had to detect, by either knocking them down or navigating around them. If your strategy was to avoid them, using a bumper or Touch Sensor would not be the ideal way to detect the walls. The Ultrasonic Sensor was perfect for this task; since the walls were rather large and flat, the sensors had little trouble detecting the walls. In Figure 7–14, you can see DemoBot with an Ultrasonic Sensor installed on the front trying to detect a LEGO wall field object. The NXT-G code shown in Figure 7–15 shows the robot using an Ultrasonic Sensor for collision detection; the robot will move forward until it detects an object in front of it and stop and turn to the right to avoid a collision.

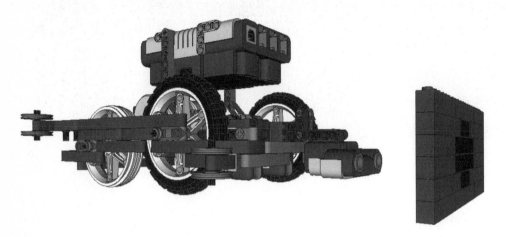

Figure 7–14. DemoBot with an Ultrasonic Sensor detecting a sensor wall

Figure 7–15. NXT-G code using an Ultrasonic Sensor for collision detection

When using an Ultrasonic Sensor on your robot, be aware of unintended objects getting in the sensor's view path. For example, during many competitions, referees or team members may have to reach onto the game field to remove a stray object. You want to be careful not to allow the robot to detect the person reaching onto the field and causing your robot to change its course thinking that it has encountered an obstacle.

Summary

Taking advantage of sensors is the best way to make a smart robot. A robot that can navigate by interpreting its environment will be much better at handling changes or differences in the game field. Things such as ripples in the field mat or game elements not in the exact same place as your practice table are less of an issue if your robot is working with sensors to locate its final goal, rather than just depending on everything being exactly like your practice field back in the classroom or at home.

PART 3

Manipulation

CHAPTER 8

■ ■ ■

Passive Attachments

Now that you have learned about how to make the robot navigate the game field, the next trick is to have the robot actually do something when it gets to its desired location. We will do this with particular attachments that will be mounted to the robot chassis and designed to help the robot carry out particular missions. A winning robot only navigates the game field effectively but it must be able to complete the game missions.

The design of attachments is twofold. First, a design needs to be such that it can actually do the desired task without error, and second, an attachment needs to be versatile enough that it can be either reused for multiple missions or designed in such a way that attaching and removing it from the robot chassis is smooth and easy to do. Attachments are the hooks, claws, collectors, or really just about anything your robot can use to complete a task. In most cases, there isn't a single attachment design that can do all the missions on a game field unless the game missions are fairly simple. In FLL events, there will normally be around ten (give or take a few) tasks that the robot must do to complete the missions, and rarely will a single tool be useful for all of these missions. Because of the fact that these tools might have to be swapped out, we must design tools that can be added and removed from our robot chassis, that is, attachments.

Once attached to our robot chassis, a tool becomes a part of the robot and must follow the same guidelines that the robot itself in regards to shape, size, and parts used. The rules that regulate the size of your robot in FLL apply to the complete size of your robot with the attachments included, not just the robot chassis. Keep the FLL design rules in mind when building attachments for your robot; it's easy to overlook them until it's too late.

Since attachments could need to be removed and added during the competition, it's best to design a solution that can be added and removed in as little time as possible. At FLL events, a team only has 2.5 minutes to complete as many of the missions as possible, and swapping out attachments on the robot in base can be one of the most time consuming things a team will do. So don't make attachments hard to put on or remove; keep them simple. Also practice over and over again the addition and removal of your robot's attachments.

LEGO robot attachments can be broken into two basic categories, either passive or powered. In this chapter, we will talk about *passive attachments*. These are attachments that do not require a motor to operate; they are simply hooked to the robot chassis and controlled by the navigation of the robot itself. *Powered attachments* will use a motor to enable to attachment to work; for most robots, their third motor will drive an attachment. Recall that in FLL your robot is allowed to use only three motors in total, and in most cases, two are used to navigate the robot. Chapter 9 will cover the design and uses of powered attachments. Powered attachments can also have a subcategory of pneumatics, where LEGO pneumatics are used to power the attachments movements instead of a LEGO NXT motor; Chapter 10 will cover the design principles of pneumatic attachments.

How do you know when you should use a passive attachment versus a powered attachment? There is no right or wrong answer to this question; it simply comes down to determining the right tool for the job. Most robot teams will use a combination of both passive and powered. One of the advantages of using a passive attachment is that most passive attachments have very simple designs and don't require an extensive amount of engineering; for a young or new team, this can be helpful.

Types of Passive Attachments

The types of passive attachments are pretty much only limited by what your imagination can dream up, but most of them will fall into one of the following categories:

- Pushing attachments
- Hooking attachments
- Dumping attachments
- Collecting attachments
- Spring-loaded attachments

Of course, some ideas will be completely outside of these general categories and there is nothing wrong with that. Again the only limitations are the game rules and what you and your team can dream up. As long as it works, there is no bad design.

When thinking of design ideas for your attachments, look to real life machines or tools that perform a similar function. For example, if you have a mission that requires you to simply push a field item, think of machines that push, such as a bulldozer or snow plow. Both of these push things but have a different-shaped blade depending on the goal for the task.

Maybe the task is to latch onto something, say a loop on the field, so you could make an attachment that is similar to a fishing hook; a hook can grab an item from one direction but not release when moving in a different direction.

Anytime you can associate a desired action with an existing tool or machine, you've saved yourself a great deal of work. Now, you just have to be able to simulate that tool in LEGO and make it applicable to your robot design. These are good things to bring up during any robot design judging that you may have at your competition; often, design judges will ask where the inspiration for your designs came from and being able to point out such similarities with existing tools or machines is a nice touch. It shows you did your homework when designing your robot and its attachments.

Pushing

One of the most common and easiest attachments to have on your robot is one that pushes. A pushing attachment can be as simple as a flat LEGO wall or something more complicated like a plow that not only pushes but clears a path. Pushing can also be about delivering something on the game field. Many times a game will have missions that require delivering something to a particular place on the game field and really the easiest way to get it there is to just push it along the mat.

Bumper

A bumper attachment is just that, a small wall that is hooked to your robot's chassis (see Figure 8–1). It doesn't have to be a big wall could be as simple as a small bumper like a car would have on the front. The idea you're going for is a flat surface on the front of your robot that you can use to run into objects. In the FLL 2010 Body Forward game, there were lots of missions that required the robot to make contact and push the field object. The pushing would result in some action happening, such a door opening or a lever lifting something up.

The attachment doesn't need to be fancy or complicated, it just needed to be able to make proper contact with the field object. You could then use the robot's drive system to push the bumper forward. With a solution such at this the programming becomes important since the drive system is not only moving the robot its causing some interaction with the field object. A delicate touch is what is needed most of the time; rarely do you want to hit something hard for fear that you'll damage the field object or the robot.

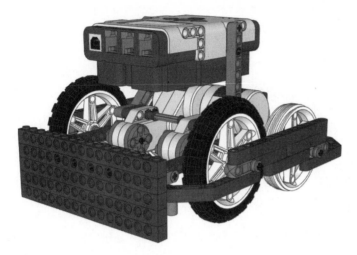

Figure 8–1. *DemoBot with a flat bumper installed*

Plow

Unlike a bumper, where you want to push an object forward, you may have the need to push something out of your way or possibly clear a path. If this is the case, you don't want a flat bumper that meets the object perpendicularly; you need something that will make impact and then push the object clear of the robot's path. Think of a snow plow; the blade on a snow plow is at an angle, and as the snow is pushed, it goes off to the side. The simple motion of the plow truck and the shape of the plow blade make this happen. The very same principle can be applied with a LEGO robot.

Just build your bumper with an angle that will move the object without much force. Depending on the object you are trying to move, the size of the angle and the force needed will differ. Don't be afraid to experiment and try different designs. Be sure to take notes of the different designs you try and include the findings in your technical documentation that you present to any design judges at your event. Being able to document why your team built something the way that you did is always good in the judge's eyes.

Your plow should have a smooth face on it as well. Don't just take a LEGO plate with studs facing forward and expect your target object to move out of the way. You want to minimize the friction by having a nice smooth surface on your plow. If you do use a LEGO plate, be sure to add some LEGO tiles to it so that any studs facing out don't cause objects to get caught or not move as you expected. The plow in Figure 8–2 keeps the smooth side of the TECHNIC beams exposed so that any objects that make contact will slide out of the way.

Figure 8–2. DemoBot with plow for pushing objects out of the path of the robot

Delivery Box

Maybe instead of trying to make contact with a field object you're trying to deliver some objects on the field. You could try to build a complicated claw or attachment that contains the objects and then opens up to release them, but many times, a simple delivery box will do. In Figure 8–3, the robot is using a four-sided box to deliver the ball; without the box, the ball could roll away from the robot.

In the FLL 2008 Climate Connections game, many objects had to be delivered to particular places on the field. The rules stated that the objects must be making contact with the field mat but there were no rules against containing or corralling the object in a box made from LEGO bricks. In order to keep with the rules about making contact with the game mat, you simply built a LEGO box that had four sides but no bottom.

The great part about this was that you just had to drop the pieces into the box that needed to be delivered and then push the box along the game field to the desired location. No special arms or fancy attachments were needed on the robot, just a way to push the box. You could have had something as easy as a bumper or something with a little more design effort that would hold the delivery box on three sides but allow the box to be release when the robot went in reverse. Just a bumper with three sides that fit around the box would be perfect and could possibility be reusable for other task as well.

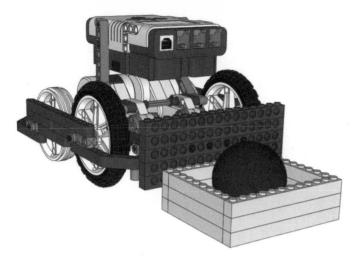

Figure 8–3. A bottomless box being pushed into place with a simple bumper attachment

---

■ **Note** Attachments that can be used for more than one task not only save you design time but can also save your team lots of competition time by avoiding the need to change out attachments.

When you build a delivery box think about how the box will travel across the game field. You will want the box to have as little friction with the mat as possible. You could put some tiny wheels on the box, but then you run the risk of having trouble if the robot needs to make turns while making the delivery, since the wheels on the box are not going to steer with your robot (they will simply skid). Adding some skids to the box would be a better idea, anything that is smooth and slides easy on the mat surface. Here you can be creative; try using TECHNIC beams on their sides or some LEGO tiles attached to the bottom of your box. Don't be afraid to use parts you would never have thought would be handy in LEGO robots events. I've seen LEGO minifig snow skis used, and they slid across the game field well. Again, just like with the plow attachment, don't be afraid to try different idea and test them out. Just be sure that you document everything so that you can show design judges how your solutions came about.

Hooking

Hooking objects and returning them to base is one of the more popular tasks on FLL game fields in recent years. Capturing loops seems to be a common mission that robots have had to perform in past years. Many teams will overthink this kind of task and build overly complicated attachments to retrieve the loops. I understand the attraction to build big and complicated for the cool factor, but this is not normally the winning design you want. Having more moving parts just means there are more things to break and go wrong with your attachment. The key to a consistent robot is keeping it simple. The fewer things that can go wrong, the better off your robot will be in the long run.

Simple Hook

To start off simple, a basic hook shaped attachment can do wonders with a little good programming behind it. The strategy will be for the robot to navigate up to the object and place the hook in such a position that when the robot moves away the field object is caught on the robot's hook and can be returned to base without falling off. In Figures 8–4 and 8–5, the robot has a simple hook attachments; once the robot moves into position, pulling the object back to base is done without great effort.

While hooking an object may sound easy, it will require a robot that can navigate very smoothly and consistently. Depending on your hook design and what you are trying to capture, there may not be a lot of room for error. Keep this in mind when deciding on your hooks design; even though the hook itself is simple, actually getting it to work each time might be a bit more of a challenge.

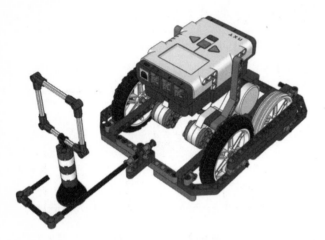

Figure 8–4. A hook attachment moving into place behind the scoring object

Figure 8–5. Once the hook is behind the object, the robot simply moves backwards to retrieve the item to base.

Fish Hook

If you look at the design of a fish hook, you will notice the end of the hook has a barb facing the opposite direction. When used on a fish, the big hook actually catches the fish, but the barb keeps the fish from slipping off the hook. This same design can be used with LEGO robot attachments as well by simply building a big hook with some kind of LEGO element on the tip that will keep anything the hook catches from slipping back off. Again, don't over think the design; just add a simple bushing or pin on the end of your hook so that the newly captured object isn't allowed to fall off the hook before you return to base with your prize.

In Figure 8–6, the steps for a robot retrieving a loop using a fish hook attachment are shown.

1. The robot faces the loop.

2. Now, it drives past the loop.

3. It turns carefully toward the loop.

4. As the robot moves backward, the hook is caught.

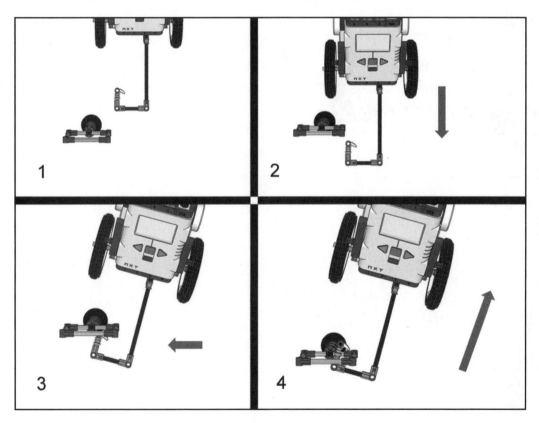

Figure 8–6. *The steps of a robot using a fish hook type attachement*

Carabineers

If you have ever gone rock climbing or seen rock climbing equipment, you have most likely seen a carabiner. These great hooks have a spring-loaded gate on them. The idea is that you the hook will only go in one direction when capturing an object. The gate on the carabiner only opens in one direction; the robot navigates to the object and forces the carabineer hook onto or over the object, allowing the gate to open when hooking the object, but when the gate closes, it will not open in the opposite direction thus holding the object on the hook.

Figure 8–7 shows a carabiner hook attachment over the loop object with the hook's latch in a closed position. In Figure 8–8, you can see the pressure from the attachment coming down on top of the loop caused the latch on the carabiner to open. Once the loop comes inside the carabineer, the latch closes around the loop and locks it in place, as shown in Figure 8–9.

Building such a hook is rather simple with LEGO bricks; you just build a hook with a gate that is held in place with a LEGO belt (you will have lots of various sizes in your LEGO MINDSTORM kit). Be sure to make the gate big enough for your object to fit through, and again, make sure there is some room for error. Don't make the opening so narrow that your object will only fit if the robot hits it perfectly. This is something you should practice repeatedly until you come up with a design that will perform without error. You may need to adjust the belt you used for your gate spring to increase or decrease the tension as well as work with the overall size of your hook.

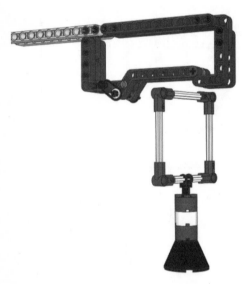

Figure 8–7. Carabiner being positioned over the loop with the latch closed

Figure 8–8. *When the carabiner makes contact with the loop, the latch opens.*

Figure 8–9. *Now the latch on the Carabiner closes, locking the loop in place.*

Fork

While, technically, the fork design is not exactly a hook, it does work well when trying to collect loops on a game field. Passive fork designs are not always effective since many times you may need to lift the loop that you are collecting and that will required a powered attachment, which I'll talk about in Chapter 9. There are times when a passive fork design will work though. If you are creative, you might even be able to design a solution where the fork is not powered but can still create lift as it moves into the loop. Figure 8–10 shows a robot with a fork attachment.

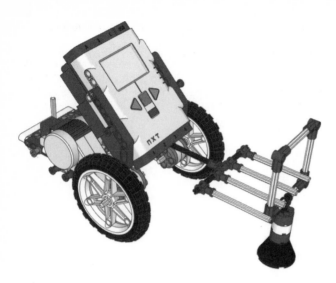

Figure 8–10. A four-prong fork attachment spearing a field object

The idea behind a fork attachment is just like a fork you would use at the dinner table. It has a set of prongs on the front and is driven into the object you are trying to capture. You will need to keep the size of the object in mind when designing your fork attachment, since the object does need to fit between the prongs on your fork. The number of prongs is also something you need to keep in mind; the more prongs you have, the more room for error you have as well. However, if you make the fork too big, you could run into navigation issues when trying to return to base with your prize.

You could also build a hybrid of the fish hook and the fork; by adding small barbs on the end of each fork prong, you can keep the object from slipping free without having to lift the fork. Again, this depends on how your game field is set up and what type of object you are trying to collect.

Dumping

At times, your robot will need to deliver an object or a group of objects that need to be put behind or on top of another object. In these cases, just pushing them across the game field will not be enough you will need to find a way to deliver them in a different way. In most cases, dumping the delivery will work. Think of machines that dump; the obvious example is a dump truck. It has a large bed on the back that lifts to let the contents slide out to a location behind the truck. The same idea can work for your robot as well.

Think of how the bed on a dump truck works: it lifts up to cause the items in the bed to dump out. But we're working with passive attachments, so we will need to find a different way to cause the dumping action to take place. Gravity will be our friend when we try to design such an attachment. The simplest way to build a dump bed is to create a tilting bed that can be locked into the load position and has a trigger that will be pushed out of the way to allow the tilting bed to fall and release the contents.

First, build the tilting bed so that it is large enough to hold all the objects you wish to deliver. Also, make sure that the surface of the tilt bed is smooth enough to allow the contents to slide out without a lot of friction. It should also be large enough so that, when the objects are sliding out of the tilt bed, they do not get jammed up against each other causing them to get stuck in the tilt bed.

Figure 8–11 shows a dump bed. It is important that the pivot point is kept far enough back that when the trigger is released, the dump bed will tilt forward enough to release the contents. The trigger is holding the bed in place, and when the trigger is pushed backward, the dump bed becomes unstable and falls forward, as shown in Figure 8–12.

The tilt bed needs to be mounted high enough on the robot chassis so that when the robot moves into place for the delivery, the contents of the tilt bed will be able to reach their destination. For example, in the FLL 2008 Climate Connections game, one of the missions was to deliver a number of items behind a short wall of LEGO bricks. In order for a tilt bed to work correctly in delivering the items, it needed to be mounted high enough to reach over the wall of LEGO bricks and still have room for the bed to tilt enough for the contents to land in the proper location.

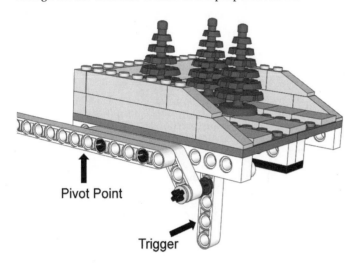

Figure 8–11. *A dump attachment carring a load of small trees with a trigger in place preventing the dump bed from releasing*

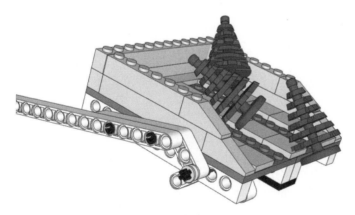

Figure 8–12. *Once the trigger is pushed backward, the dump bed falls forward and releases the load of small trees.*

The tilting action itself will be done by taking advantage of potential energy that is stored in the tilt bed by locking it in place with a lever or pin.

■ **Note** *Potential energy* is energy that is stored within a system. It exists when there is a force that tends to pull an object back toward some lower energy position. This force is often called a *restoring force*. For example, when a rubber band is stretched to the left, it exerts a force to the right so as to return to its original, unstretched position. Similarly, when a mass is lifted up, the force of gravity will act to bring it back down. The action of stretching the rubber band or lifting the mass requires energy to perform. The energy that went into lifting up the mass is stored in its position in the gravitational field, and the energy it took to stretch the rubber band is stored in the rubber.

Now, the energy we used to lift the tilt bed in place is storing energy for tilting when the lever or pin holding it in place is removed. The balance of the tilting bed should be designed in such a way that when the bed is in not being held in place by a lever or pin, it will return quickly to the dump state. To adjust the balance of your tilt bed, you just need to move the position of the fulcrum. If gravity is not enough to tilt the bed as desired, a spring can be added by using a LEGO belt attached to the tilting bed. When the bed is in delivery state, the belt is stretched, and once the trigger is pressed, the energy bound in the belt will release and cause the bed to dump its load.

The trigger for your dump bed will be located in such a way that when the robot arrives at the desired delivery location, the trigger will be pressed. Just like with other passive attachments, be sure to make the trigger big enough that you have plenty of room for error. You don't want to make the trigger so small or difficult to activate that you decrease your chances of completing the mission correctly each time.

Now, for your robot to make the delivery, you load up the items into your tilt bed while the robot is sitting in base. Then, the robot navigates to the desired dumping zone or location. Drive forward until the tilt bed trigger is pushed and the tilt bed releases and dumps its contents in the proper location.

Collecting

Many LEGO robot challenges will require robots to collect field objects and bring them back to base or deliver them to other locations on the field. The hook attachment we talked about previously is one kind of attachment that can be used for collecting particular objects that have a handle or loop that the hook can latch onto. Sometimes, the objects you are trying to collect might be shaped in such a way that they have nothing for you to hook onto, so you will need some other designs for your passive collectors.

One-Way Box

A ball can be of the trickier things to try to collect on a game field. Balls don't have anything we can grab with a hook, and they tend to roll away when we try to push them. Building a one-way box for collecting such items is a good solution. For this attachment, you have a box with three stationary sides and a forth wall that is a flap that only opens in one direction, allowing balls to enter the box but not to leave.

With such an attachment, your robot can navigate around the game field pushing the one-way box attachment into the path of the objects you wish to collect, such as balls. When building the opening side of the box, be sure to build it large enough to be able to capture your objects and still have room for the flap to open again without any of the previously collected items jamming the flap and preventing it from opening.

In Figure 8–13, the robot is pushing a three-sided box with a flap on the front that is kept shut by gravity. It has a stop on it that allows the flap to open only inward (it prevents the flap from opening in the outward direction), thus keeping us from loosing anything that we capture. Figure 8–14 demonstrates how the ball will push past the flap and enter the box as the robot moves forward. Now, the ball is trapped in the attachment and cannot escape even if the robot drives backward, as shown in Figure 8–15.

The flap on your attachment can either be spring loaded with a LEGO belt or just use gravity to stay closed when no objects are entering the box. First, try using the attachment with just gravity closing the flap. If the collected objects tend to escape after being collected, you may need to add a spring to the door to force it closed faster. Be careful not to make the tension on the flap so tight that objects trying to enter the box are pushed away instead of being captured.

Figure 8–13. The robot approaches the ball with an ball collector attachment.

Figure 8–14. As the robot moves forward, the ball pushes its way into the attachment.

Figure 8–15. Once the ball enters the attachment, the door swings closed behind it, locking it inside.

Another variation on the one-way box would be to have just a lip on the front of the box instead of a flap. By adding a plate or axle across the front of the box, you can prevent some items from exiting the collection box as long as the robot continues to roll forward. Be careful though, if the robot moves backward quickly or for a long distance, the objects you have collected in the box can get free.

Sweeper

A sweeper is similar to the one-way box in principle, but instead of having a simple flap on the front of the box, you add a more complicated apparatus. The idea might be similar to a vacuum cleaner; there would be a set of spinning brushes or blades on the front of the box. The spinning motion could be activated by a wheel on the outside of the box that is attached to the drive axle of your sweeper. As the robot navigates the field, the wheel rolls along the mat and transfers the motion to the sweeper bushes or blades.

This kind of attachment can be very handy when trying to collects lots of small items that tend to roll away easily or are hard to collect with hooks or bumpers. Most of the time, sweeper attachments are rather large, so keep the overall size of your robot in mind when you build this type of attachment. You do not want to exceed the size limits. Also, these types of attachments require a good bit of testing and reengineering to get working properly, but they can be a great way to collect multiple of objects of various sizes at one time.

Figure 8–16 shows a robot with a sweeper attachment. As the robot moves forward, the wheel will turn the gears that cause the sweeper arms to rotate and push items into the attachment.

Figure 8–16. A sweeper attachment for collecting field items

As I noted before, attachments that can be used for many different tasks are best, since they will save time and effort on the game field. So if your game rules require you to do a lot of collecting on the field, a sweeper of some kind might be an ideal solution.

Spring-Loaded Attachments

Many times, you may want an attachment that performs a power function, but you don't want to use a motor as the source of the power. Using springs or LEGO belts is a great way to get an attachment to perform an action without using a motor.

LEGO belts are, for the most part, fancy rubber bands. Now think of what happens when you pull a rubber band back on your finger and let go at one end? It shoots across the room, because when you pull the rubber band back and stretch it out, you are storing energy in the rubber band, and when you release one end of the rubber band, you are releasing the energy that was stored. With a LEGO belt, you can use the same principle (but do not shoot them like rubber bands; they will break). Figure 8–16 shows that with just a few parts, a powerful flipper can be created. Figure 8–17 shows the flipper compressed against the field table wall, and Figure 8–18 shows the flipper after the robot has turned and released it.

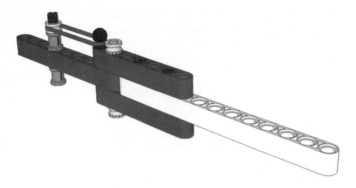

Figure 8–17. *A flipper that can be attached to a robot chassis and then pulled back to be released for triggering field objects*

Figure 8–18. *A flipper compressed with the game table wall*

Figure 8–19. Robot releasing the flipper by turning away from the wall, releasing the compressed flipper

With passive attachments, you can build flippers that are bound to a belt and pulled back and locked in place with a trigger. For example, if you have a mission object that needs to be knocked off its base, a flipper attachment would be ideal for doing this. The robot starts in base with the flipper locked and loaded. Then it navigates to the field object. When the trigger is released by bumping into a particular element on the field (or the table wall), the trigger will be released, and the energy from the belt will cause the attachment to flip quickly and strike the object that you are hoping to hit.

The drawback with this type of attachment is that you only get one use of the flipper per trip from base, since the attachment cannot reload itself and must be manually loaded in base by a team member.

Attachment Interfaces

Now that you have a collection of attachments, you need a way to hook them onto your robot chassis quickly, and you need to be able to remove them just as quickly. As noted before, adding and removing an attachment is one of the biggest time killers for a team when competing. Think of a race car pit crew; when the car comes for a pit stop, the team must work quickly to change out the tires, add fuel, and even clean the windshield. The same is true for when your robot returns to base and your team has to switch out attachments. The team must be well rehearsed in the changing process, and the attachments need to be design in such a way that allows for easy removal and addition.

Making up a system that allows for the attachments to come on and off the robot is very important. With passive attachments, the interface can be very simple, since you do not have to worry about motor attachments. If you are using both powered and passive attachments on your robot, keep in mind that you may need to design an attachment interface that will accept both types.

Snapping Pins

Using TECHNIC pins is the most common way to connect attachments to your robot chassis and works well as long as you keep the design simple and easy to access. You don't want to fumble with hard-to-access pins or pin holes when trying to connect your attachment to the robot. Remember, saving time is the main goal, so keep everything easy to access and see. If you can use the same pin layout for all your attachments, thus creating a universal interface as shown in Figure 8–20, you will make the process of adding and removing attachments much more streamlined. And when you add new attachment designs using the same universal interface, the learning curve is reduced everyone on the team. If all your team members are familiar with the interface you've been using to connect your previous attachments, adding a new attachment that uses the same interface will be less confusing for everyone.

Figure 8–20. A set of front mounted pins for quick attaching and releasing of attachments

Nonsnapping Pins

Some attachments can be connected to a chassis without having to be hard attached; they can simply be held in place by gravity and some nonsnapping pins. To use this type of interface, you have a set of nonsnapping pins made from something as simple as a TECHNIC axle that just rest in some holes on the robot chassis. Nothing is truly snapped in place; it's just set in place and held by the weight of the attachment itself. If this type of interface works for your attachments, adding and removing attachments can be done very quickly without having to snap or unsnap anything. Again, the goal is speed. Figure 8–20 shows a bumper attachment with non-snapping pins being connected to the robot chassis.

Figure 8–21. *Nonsnapping pins slip into holes on the beam to allow the attachment to quickly connect to the robot chassis.*

Magnets

Even thought they don't come in the MINDSTORM kit, LEGO does make magnets and magnet holders. LEGO train sets are a great source for these magnets (the trains use them as couplers between cars). They can be used on your robot as a coupler for connecting attachments as well. The magnets are very strong, and depending on the size of your attachment, you may be able to use the magnets alone. If you require a bit more support, you can use the magnets along with the nonsnapping pin system: the pins guide the attachment into place on your robot chassis and the magnets hold everything tightly in place. Figure 8–21 shows a pair of LEGO train magnets installed.

Figure 8–22. A pair of LEGO train magnets mounted to the front of DemoBot for quick attachment

Summary

All of these passive attachment designs are purely suggestions; there is truly no limit to the number of designs that can be created to complete LEGO robotics task. Don't be afraid to experiment and try new designs or mix together design ideas. The keys to a good attachment—both active and passive—are reusability, quick addition and removal, and predictability.

CHAPTER 9

■■■

Power Attachments

In chapter 8, you learned why having attachments on our robots are necessary for our robots to complete their missions. And although passive attachments can be very helpful, sometimes, our robot attachments need a bit more horsepower. By adding power to our attachments, we can have a wide range of new functions that our robot can now perform, such as grabbing, lifting, triggering, and even pushing. On the NXT brick, there are only three power outlets, and for most robot designs, two of the outputs will be used for navigation. This leaves only one power source for attachments, so we must use it wisely. Just like with the passive attachments, the idea of having a common interface for fast attachment switching is important. There may be times when you have missions that need a claw attachment and later you find the need for an attachment to lift an object. These attachments need to connect to the NXT server so that they can be switched quickly with very little effort. Later in this chapter, we will discuss some common interface designs.

In FIRST LEGO League, teams are allowed to bring only three motors to the competition table, so those teams cannot have attachments with their own motors. All power attachments will need to share a single motor. This rule may not be the case with all robotics events, so be sure to consult your game rules regarding having multiple attachment motors.

Power Attachment Locations

When we designed our robot's chassis, among our considerations were where we would connect our attachments and where the motor for the attachments would be located if we decide to use power attachments. Not only do we have to have room for our attachment motor but we now need to think about how the third motor will affect the center of gravity and balance of our robot chassis. The attachment motor can be located in various places on our robot—on the front of the robot, in the center or even in the rear—depending what our attachments will be expected to do and how they will be incorporated into our robot design.

Adding an Attachment to the Front

The most common location for an attachment motor is the front of the robot, and for most designs, this will work perfectly. Just be aware of how this effects the balance of your robot, not only when its sitting still but when the robot is in motion and when it comes to a stop. And if your attachment is grabbing or collecting an object, the weight of the collected object will also need to be considered. You'd hate to have a perfectly balanced robot when it has no load but then find that your robot is unstable after collecting a field object. Figure 9–1 shows the DemoBot with a front-mounted attachment motor.

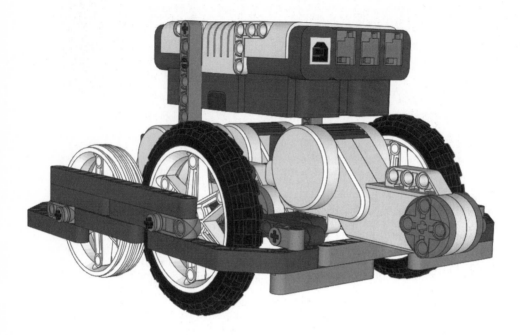

Figure 9–1. DemoBot with an attachment motor mounted on the front

If your robot is using bumpers or other sensors located on the front of the chassis be careful to not let your attachment motor interfere with the expected performance of the sensors. Also be aware of the wires paths on your robot, once a lot of items such as motors and sensor get into the same location the wires can get a bit tight.

Adding an Attachment to the Center

By locating our attachment in the center of the robot chassis, we make it much easier to maintain our center of gravity. If the motor is mounted in the middle by adding some clever gearing we can create multiple motion paths for the attachments. The idea is that we could have vertical motion and horizontal motion from the same motor without having to switch out any parts.

In Figure 9–2, the attachment motor is mounted in the middle with the NXT motor on its side, which mean the path of motion is a front-to-back horizontal one. By adding a pair of bevel gears or a bevel gear box, the path of motion can be allowed to be vertical as well, as shown in Figure 9–3.

Figure 9–2. LEGO robot with a NXT motor mounted in the middle on its side

Figure 9–3. A middle-mounted NXT motor connected to a bevel gear box to change the direction of the motor's output

Adding an Attachment to the Rear

A more uncommon location for an attachment motor can be in the rear of the robot chassis, like the one shown in Figure 9–4. One of the biggest advantages of this can be in using the attachment motor as a counter weight. If we know our robot is going to have issues with tipping forward when carrying heavy objects, having a rear-mounted attachment motor can help add the necessary counterweight to keep the robot from falling forward. The drawback is that the axle has to be brought forward for the attachment to make used of the motor's motion.

Figure 9–4. A rear-mounted attachment motor helps balance a front-heavy robot design

Types of Attachments

When considering the type of attachment that is needed for the mission, think of the movements you would make with your own hands. Would you grab the object, or would lifting it up be even better? Maybe just a gentle push is needed. Once you've thought through the movement necessary, think of modern machines that do these very same actions. We have forklifts or cranes with claws for picking up objects. Excavators with large attachments grab and move objects. All of these things can be inspiration for your team when building power attachments.

Attachments That Grab

One of the basic functions for an attachment is to grab something. Oftentimes, game missions will require an object to be captured and returned to base or another location on the game field. Just as you could use your hand to simply grab the object, your robot can do the same. And by using powered attachments the speed, duration, and strength of the grab can be controlled. This gives us an advantage over passive attachments that cannot control such elements of the grab.

Claw

The claw is one of the most common of LEGO robotics attachments. The design concept is very much that of a claw in the real world. Think of the claw on a crab; it has two opposing jaws that share a hinge point and when the jaws are moved toward each other, they compress any objects inside the claw. That's kind of a fancy way of saying the claw will squeeze whatever is inside of its pinchers.

For a robot claw, the concept is very much the same. A claw consists of at least two jaw-like elements that are hinged: either all jaws would move, or one is stationary and the others move. The attachment motor drives the moving elements from the hinge point and forces the claw to grab whatever is within its grasp.

Figure 9–5 shows a claw design driven by a series of gears on the hinge. The motor turns the gear on first pincher, and the second gear drives the other pincher in the opposite direction of the first, causing the claw to grab or release. The actual claw elements are forced in toward each other and will grab the object.

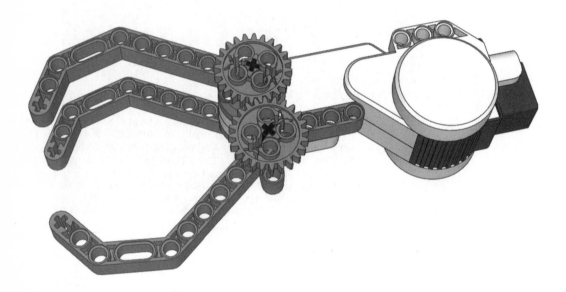

Figure 9–5. Claw design that where both pinchers are driven by the NXT motor.

You will need to add some logic in the NXT-G code to indicate when to stop closing the claw motion. Using time as duration will be sufficient in most cases. If there is a greater need for the claw to sense when its grabbed an object, adding touch sensors to the claw could be an option (but will most likely be over engineering for most LEGO robots).

Vise Grip

The vise grip attachment is very similar to a claw, but the motion used for closing the vice grip is much different. With the claw, the two sides are hinged the same pivot point, but with a vise grip, you have a set of jaws are not hinged at all. Instead, they are designed to move in a linear motion when closing.

Think of a vise on a workbench, when the spindle is turned, the jaws either closer together or move further apart.

The same design can be used with a LEGO vise grip attachment like the one shown in Figure 9–6. Using a set of worm gears, we could build a long threaded spindle that, when turned by a NXT motor, would be able to either close or open our attachment jaws. The nice thing about a vise grip attachment is that if you are trying to pick up something that is a bit delicate or requires a light touch, the vice grip will a better choice over the claw. The vice grip allows for a bit more precision in the amount of force being applied when grabbing an object, and the squeezing motion is more even because the motion is linear instead of at an angle, as it is with a claw.

Figure 9–6. *Vise grip attachment*

When programming the vise grip, it will be helpful to know the size of the object you are attempting to grab. This will allow you to be able to preprogram the duration needed for the motor to run while clamping down on the object. Since the vise grip could be using worm gears for the spindle, and these types of gears are not very forgiving when over torqued, they could cause your attachment to bust. This would be a good time to use a torque gear like we talked about in Chapter 2. The torque gear would allow your attachment motor to run a bit more than needed without risking breaking the attachment or the object you're attempting to collect.

Trap

Another way to grab something would be to trap it. Think of a baseball player. When a player makes a catch in a glove, the coach will say to bring the other hand over quickly and trap the ball in the glove. Otherwise, the ball could fall out again. With LEGO robots, we can make an attachment that works in the same way. The robot will move into place, capture the desired object in the open trap, and then close the trap using a motor to hold the object in place.

The great thing about a trap attachment is that is can be used not only for capturing objects but for delivering them as well. Plus it's not limited to capturing a single object like a claw or vise attachment. The trap attachment can round up various objects of different sizes and shapes without much effort. This attachment can be a big box that can be open and shut as you need using the motor. In Figures 9–7 and 9–8, you can see a capture box that opens in the middle to capture objects. This is a bit different that the passive box attachment that only traps incoming objects but has no way to release the object when needed, so the powered attachment is much more helpful in delivery.

Figure 9–7. Trap box that can capture multiple objects of various sizes

Figure 9–8. Trap attachment closed with captured objects inside

If the plan is to use the trap for multiple captures, make sure you build it big enough so that objects already captured don't get in the way or escape when you capture your subsequent ones.

Attachments That Lift

In many events, the missions will require multiple types of attachments to complete the entire list of tasks, so although grabbing things might get you far, you might need to lift objects as well. Many times, the objects are inside of or behind other field objects, so to retrieve these objects, you will need to carefully lift them out of their locations without breaking or damaging the surroundings.

And with LEGO elements, "gentle" is sometimes the key word. You don't get credit for returning to base with only a piece of the object; you need to bring back the entire thing. This was the case in the 2009 FLL Smart Moves game, where one of the missions was to retrieve loops off the top of vertically mounted TECHNIC axles. If you tried to grab the loops and pull them off, they would break. The only clean way to retrieve them was to actually lift them off their perches.

Just like attachments that grab, there are several variations of attachments that can lift. I will cover some of the basics designs, but don't limit your thinking to this list. Look around at everyday tools and machines, and study how they operate; many of these designs can be incorporated into a good LEGO attachment. Also, be sure to document where your inspiration came from; these are the kinds of things the technical judges like to hear.

Lever

When you need to create a lifting motion, the easiest way is to simply create a lever mounted to the NXT motor. Even though this design is very simple, it is also very effective. Remember that complicated is not always the best choice when it comes to a LEGO robot; simple works well.

A lever design is nothing more than having a lifting arm of some sort with a rotation point located at the power source. The motion is rotational, because the lever lifts, so you have to be careful to control the duration of the lift or your lever will make a complete circle, or at least try to.

Also since your lifting motion is rotational, the object you're lifting will need to be attached in such a way that the changing angle of your level won't drop or release the captured object. As you can surmise from Figure 9–9, at different degrees of lifting the angle of the object being lifted will change. Make sure your attachment is designed with this in mind, because it can be very frustrating to lift the mission object from its location only to drop it before you return with it to base.

Figure 9–9. *Lever attachment for lifting objects*

Forklift

A forklift design is based off a forklift that you would see in any modern warehouse. The forklift's lifting motion is vertical instead of rotational, like the lever's. This will keep the object you are collecting evenly balanced while you lift it and will help keep it from being lost before you can return to base.

The vertical motion also helps when retrieving objects that are located in tight spots behind other objects that can't be disturbed. In the 2008 FLL Climate Connections game, a loop needed to be retrieved out of a tight hole. If you used a lever to retrieve the loop, you ran the risk of breaking the loop, because the rotation motion of the lever caused the loop to press against its container. However, using a vertical motion to retrieve the loop kept the loop from stressing itself on the container and prevented it from breaking.

Building a forklift attachment requires a bit more effort and design time than the lever. You will need to build up a gear system that can convert the rotational motion of your motor to a vertical motion. We already did something similar to this when we designed a vise grip earlier in this chapter. Instead of making the motion horizontal, we just need to make it move vertically. Using a spindle made from LEGO worm gears would be ideal. Not only will the worm gears allow us to pick up heavy loads, but the smooth motion of the worm gears keeps our cargo steady as we lift. In Figure 9–10, you can see a gear design that could be used on a forklift type attachment.

Figure 9–10. In this forklift-type powered attachment, as the worm gears turn, the forks will raise or lower depending on the motors direction.

Attachments That Push

Besides lifting and grabbing, your robot may need to push things. You learned in Chapter 8 that pushing can be done easily with passive attachments such as a bumper on the front of the robot chassis. However, there are times where we don't necessarily want the pushing action to come from the robot moving forward; it might be much better if the robot is stationary and the pushing action happens independently of the robot moving. Also, the pushing action may need to happen in a different direction than the one in which the robot is facing. In many cases, the robot will roll up next to the desired target and need to push the object from the side.

No matter what the case, you can build a power attachments that can convert the rotary motion of the NXT motor into a linear motion; this is called an actuator. You have already seen some examples of this type of conversion from rotary to linear in our vise grip and forklift examples. Now, we look at type of actuators that we can use for pushing objects or that can be expanded on to reach out and grab items.

The LEGO Actuator

Recently, LEGO introduced a LEGO actuator that is included in their Power Functions system (see Figure 9–11). The actuator itself is not powered, so it is allowed to be used in FLL events. The LEGO actuator can extend to a length of five LEGO studs, about 1.6 inches. It has an internal torque gearing system that will prevent over extending, and about 26 full turns are needed to extend the actuator completely. The actuator is not included in any LEGO MINDSTORMS kits, so this is something you'd have to buy separately from LEGO.

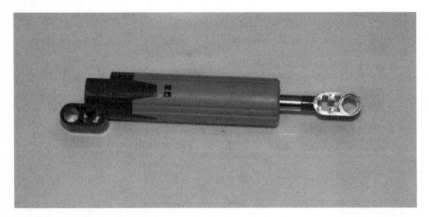

Figure 9–11. LEGO Power Functions actuator

To work the LEGO actuator, you simply attach your LEGO NXT motor to the rear of the actuator and rotate the motor in a forward motion to extend the actuator, as shown in Figure 9–12. To make the actuator contract, you just rotate the motor backward. This is a great new element from LEGO, and I believe you will see it become more and more popular in LEGO robotics as teams discover its existence.

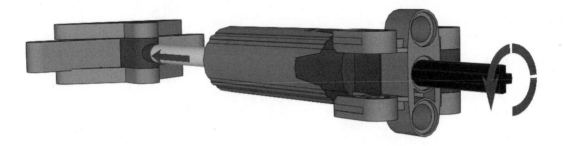

Figure 9–12. The LEGO Power Functions actuator extends as the rear shaft is turned.

Using the LEGO actuator to drive an attachment is great for movements that need to be slow and precise. Recall that the actuator extends only 1.6 inches and takes 26 motor rotations to get there. That ratio of 1.6 inches to 26 turns tell you that this motion is a slow-moving action, which is good for missions that need smooth slow pushing. The 2010 FLL Body Forward challenge was full of just such missions. At least five missions on this challenge can be done with pushing, and a few of them require slow pushing. Trying to get slow precision pushing with the bumper of a robot is not going to be easy, but you can pull up to the mission object with your robot and then activate the actuator to slowly push the item as needed with full control over the speed and force. Figure 9–13 shows an actuator connected to the front of the robot chassis that can allow for a nice, smooth pushing action.

Figure 9–13. *LEGO Power Functions actuator mounted to a robot as a pushing power attachment.*

A hook, such as we talked about in Chapter 8, could also be added to the end of the LEGO actuator for grabbing items close to the robot. This, again, would allow for a little more precision when trying capturing objects that need a more finesse than brute force.

Custom Actuator

You don't have to buy the LEGO actuator element to have an actuator on your robot. Building your own out of LEGO elements included in your LEGO MINDSTORMS kit is possible. Plus, if you need to create a motion that is linear and fast, building your own actuator is the way to go.

With just a simple combination of a LEGO spur gear and a set of LEGO gear racks, you can put together a very handy actuator. The concept just requires having the gear racks on your actuator and having the spur gear attached to the motor drive the rack gears either forward or backward. The forward motion will push the actuator out, and reversing the motion will pull it back in. Figure 9–14 shows a custom-made actuator.

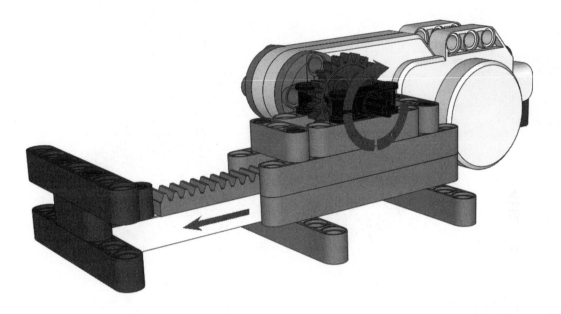

Figure 9–14. *In this custom LEGO acutator, the turning gear will push out the beam with the rack gears.*

The speed and length of your actuator is solely based on the size gears you use and how long you make the actuator. If you need to make a quick actuator, one that almost punches the target, using a larger gear to drive the actuator would be a good idea. You will need to be careful to not overextend your actuator, or else you may end up launching the entire attachment onto the game field.

If you're worried about overextending, build a stop on your actuator that will prevent it from extending beyond its reach. Then, replace the spur gear with a torque gear so that the motor will not continue to force the actuator once it's reached its stopping point. Figure 9–15 shows a custom actuator with a stop and a torque gear used to drive it.

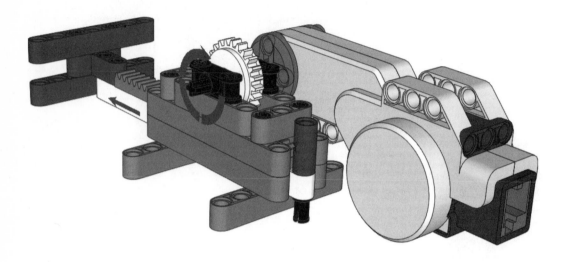

Figure 9–15. A custom LEGO acutator using a torque gear and a stop on the end of the beam to prevent the beam from overextending

Power Interfaces

Just as we talked about in Chapter 8, adding and removing attachments from your robot can be where teams lose the majority of their time during a competition. If you are participating in an FLL event, you only have 2.5 minutes at the game table to run your robot. If you spend a total of 60 seconds switching out attachments, that doesn't leave much time for completing the missions and acquiring a good game score.

The attachment methods we covered in Chapter 8 also work with power attachment. Power attachments have the extra element of the motor, so not only do you need to be able to connect or disconnect from the chassis but you need to consider how your attachment will be connected to the power source. This could be either a direct connection to the NXT motor or via some form of drive system.

Direct Connections

The most common way to connect attachments to the NXT motor is just to connect the attachment directly to the axle or pins on the NXT motor. Many teams use this method, but it's not always the most effective just because of the time it can take to add or remove attachments from the motor. Normally, anything attached directly to the motor will to difficult to remove quickly, either because of where the motor is located or how the attachment is actually connected to it.

Try to locate your attachment motor in easy-access position on your robot, where team members can get their hands in quickly and be unobstructed by wires or other parts of the robot; doing so will greatly reduce the time needed to switch out an attachment directly connected to the motor.

Also, by using easy-to-remove TECHNIC pins, such as the long pin with bushing stop shown in Figure 9–16, you can help make removing an attachment faster, because the bushing on the ends of the pins will help team members get a better grip on them for removal.

Figure 9–16. A TECNIC long pin with stop bushing

The attachment shown in Figure 9–17 is connected directly to the NXT motor with a set of easy-to-remove pins; the pins are located in such a way that they're easy to access for quick removal.

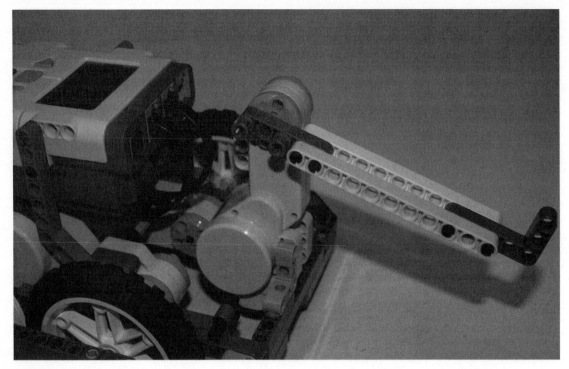

Figure 9–17. Two TECNIC long pins with stop bushing used to quickly attach a lever attachment

Gears

Connecting attachments to the power source with gears is a fast system for easy removal and adding. With gears, you don't have to have a direct connection as long as the gear on the motor or power source meshes properly with the gear on your attachment.

One approach is to design your robot with a gear connected to the motor that is exposed in such a way that attachments can connect to it. Simply speaking, the robot attachment motor will have a gear system connected to the attachment motor; this can be a single gear or a gang of gears depending on your design. On your attachment, you will also have a matching gear that is configured so that it will mesh with the motor gear when the attachment is connected to the robot.

You still need a way to connect the attachment to your robot though, and any of the ideas presented in Chapter 8 will work for power attachments as well; the only difference is that now we're adding a way for the attachment motor to connect up with the attachment and transfer power to the attachment as needed.

The sample attachment in Figure 9–18 uses a set of pins to connect the attachment to the robot chassis. When the attachment is snapped in place, the gear on the attachment lines up with the powered gear on the robot. This will provide a fast and effective method for adding the power attachment without costing the team lots of time making the change out.

Figure 9–18. *This gear interface allows for quick attachments that connect to the NXT motor.*

Driveshaft

Much like the gear method for attaching power to an attachment, you can design an accessory drive shaft on your robot. This is a shaft that is driven by your attachment motor that will allow anything connected to it to receive power from the accessory motor on the robot. This works similarly to a farm tractor that has a drive shaft on the rear for accessory. The farmer can hook up a lawn mower attachment to the shaft one day to cut grass and, the next day, attach a ground tiller to the shaft to till a field. By switching out the attachments to the drive shaft, the tractor can tackle a bunch of different tasks or missions. This concept works the same for your robot.

Adding an accessory driveshaft to your robot is very basic. The key is to make sure the location of the shaft, where attachments will connect, is a place that is universal for your attachments. Just as with the other power attachment interfaces, the key is to place the driveshaft in such a way that it's easy to access, where it's not obstructed and parts can connect and release without much effort.

In Figure 9–19, you can see an attachment that is connected to the power source via a driveshaft. When the shaft is rotated to the left, the attachment opens; when the shaft turns to the right, the attachment closes.

Figure 9–19. Driveshaft interface that connects the attachment to the power source

Summary

The goal with any attachment interfaces is to speed up the time it takes to add or remove powered attachments to your robot. Time is always the one thing that robot teams never seem to have enough of during an event.

A good point to note is that removing attachments from a robot is easier than adding them. When you design your game strategy, try to start out with as many attachments already on the robot as possible and remove them as you complete the necessary task. This will not be possible with every attachment, but the more you can start with at the beginning, the more time you can save over all. After you have all your missions worked out and the attachments designed, think of ways to maximize your designs and see if any of the attachments can be combined or even reworked so you can handle multiple tasks with a single attachment, instead of having a single attachment for each mission.

I know, when working on a team, that it's easy for a large number of attachments to get built since different groups of people may be working separately on different missions and the attachment designs may be independent of the other groups' efforts. This is a good opportunity to work as a team to refactor the designs you have and consolidate the attachments for maximum affectivity.

CHAPTER 10

■ ■ ■

Pneumatics

In the world of LEGO robotics, pneumatics are among the great mysteries to many robot teams. Since so many people either don't understand their potential, or maybe just are not aware of their existence, these parts rarely get used on LEGO robotics projects. "Pneumatics" refers to the use of pressurized gas (in LEGO, that gas is air) to create a mechanical motion.

Pneumatics give the robot another power source of manipulation besides LEGO NXT servos. Many times, a team will find that it needs an extra powered attachment that can't be created using the robot's existing attachment servo. Maybe the servo is being used for other attachments, or its location on the robot chassis doesn't work for the attachment idea that the team has in mind for a particular mission. The LEGO pneumatics can give a team this extra source of power for that attachment. LEGO pneumatics are also very strong; tasks that may cause a mechanized attachment with gears to slip, such as heavy lifting, can be done with pneumatics much easier.

Pneumatics are not for everyone, and I advise against using them just for the sake of having them on the robot. If you do use them, be sure to understand why you chose to do so, and be ready to explain this to the technical judges. In this chapter, we will talk about the how each of the components work in the system.

Operation of Pneumatic Parts

LEGO pneumatics use compressed air to push pneumatic actuators either open or closed. The air is compressed by using the LEGO pneumatic pump to fill the air tank with compressed air; this air is then released via a pneumatic air switch that directs the air to the actuators. The compressed air now forces the actuator to open or closed depending on what direction the air was put into it.

Figure 10–1 shows the flow of the air to cause an actuator to open. The steps for this circuit are as follows:

1. The pump pushes the air into the tank.

2. The switch is opened and releases the air into the lines.

3. The air causes the actuator to open.

For the actuator to close, the same process is followed, but instead of the switch pushing the air to the bottom of the actuator, the air is released into the top of the actuator, thus causing it to close. You determine whether the air makes an actuator open or close by connecting the air hose to either the open or close port. However, not all LEGO pneumatic actuators have a close port on them. Some can be only opened by air and have to be closed manually.

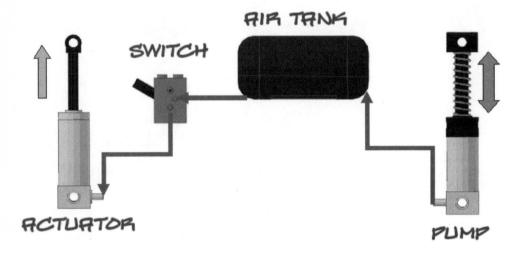

Figure 10–1. *Typical air flow of a LEGO pnuematic system*

Available Pneumatic Parts

LEGO has created a variety of pneumatic parts over the years. There are air tanks, air hoses, switches, t-joints, and actuators. While the color and size of these parts has varied, the way they work has stayed consistent.

The availability of pneumatic parts fluctuates. LEGO Education is the best source for finding the current LEGO pneumatic parts, but a variety of third party vendors sell older LEGO pneumatic parts on the Internet. A quick search on any of the popular online classifies or auction sites will most likely return a good list of parts. Be careful to make sure that any parts you use are made by LEGO. Figure 10–2 shows many of the common LEGO pneumatic parts.

Figure 10–2. *Some common LEGO pneumatic parts*

Pumps

Pumps are the primary source of air in a pneumatic circuit. There are two types of LEGO pneumatic pumps: a large manual pump that has an easy-to-activate plunger and is spring loaded and a small pump that requires a bit more effort to work manually but can be connected to a power source, such as an NXT servo, for automatic pumping. For most competitive robots, having an automatic pumping system will not be necessary, because the use of the air will be isolated to just a few missions that should be doable on just one full tank. In that case, the normal procedure would be to fill the air tank while the robot is still located in base. Figure 10–3 shows a large pneumatic pump and a small pump.

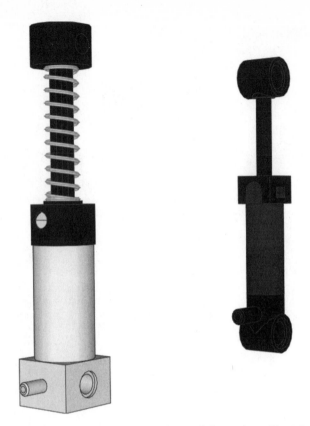

Figure 10–3. LEGO pneumatic pumps large (left) and small (right)

Air Tank

To store air for later use, a pneumatic air storage tank is available. The LEGO air tank will store the air as we compress it using the LEGO pneumatic pump. LEGO air pressure gauges are available, but for the most the most part, you can tell when the tank is getting full based on the effort required to push the pump. The tank has a hose connection on both ends: one will be used to attach the air pump and the second opening will be the output line connected to the air switch. Figure 10–4 shows a standard LEGO pneumatic air tank.

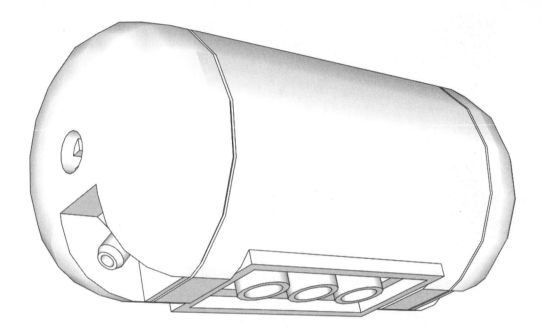

Figure 10–4. LEGO pneumatic air tank

Pneumatic Switches

Like the LEGO pneumatic pumps, LEGO pneumatic switches come in two versions, but they both work the same way. They just have different enclosures that allow for multiple ways to connect them to your robot chassis. The switches have three air connections on them and a TECHNIC-type axle connected that controls the flow of the air between the air connections on the switch. Figures 10–5, 10–6, and 10–7 show the state of the air connections based on the position of the switch. When a connection is open, the air is free to flow in or out. When a connection is closed, the air cannot escape or enter the connection. When connections are opened together, the air can flow between the open connections.

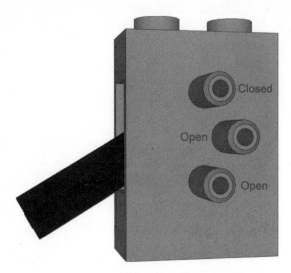

Figure 10–5. This LEGO air switch in the down position opens the middle and lower ports.

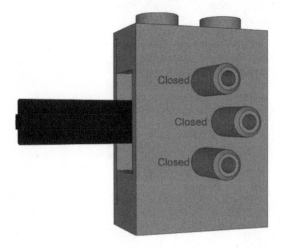

Figure 10–6. This LEGO air switch in the middle position closes all ports.

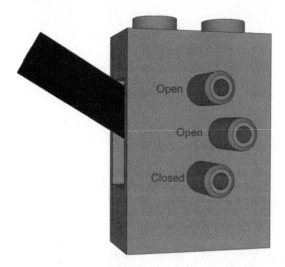

Figure 10–7. This LEGO air switch in the up position opens the middle and upper ports.

Pneumatic Actuators

The pneumatic actuator is the part that actually makes use of the compressed air. The air is used to either extend or retract the actuator. There are multiple versions of the pneumatic actuators; some have only one input, and others have a top and bottom input, as shown in Figure 10–8.

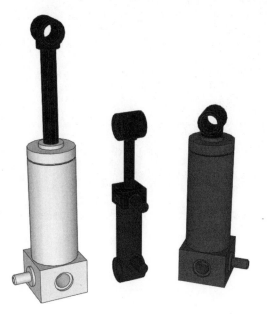

Figure 10–8. LEGO pneumatic actuators

The single-input actuators have only one input that will extend the actuator; the cylinder has to be compressed manually either by hand or with some type of spring. The more commonly used actuator available currently is the dual-input actuator, which has inputs on the top and bottom of the actuator. The bottom input will extend the cylinder, and the top input will cause the cylinder to close.

T-Joints and Air Hoses

The T-joint, shown in Figure 10–9, allows you to combine airflow from two lines into one single line or to split airflow from a single line into two. If more directions are needed, multiple T-joints can be combined to create more directions for the airflow.

LEGO air hoses are one of the few LEGO pieces that you can modify in most LEGO robotics competitions; most events allow you to cut the air hoses to the desired length. It is best to not cut any hoses until you have tested out your pneumatic attachment completely, since once the hose is cut, you can't make it longer again. The hoses you use do need to be LEGO pneumatic hoses for most robotic events.

Figure 10–9. Pneumatic T-joints connected to air hoses

Air Gauges

One of the newer LEGO pneumatic parts is a LEGO air gauge (see Figure 10–10). The gauge has a single input and a reading that goes between 0 psi (pounds per square inch) and 60 psi. Most LEGO air pumps can only reach 35–40 psi. The air gauge is not a requirement on a robot attachment, but it is nice to have for making sure your pneumatic attachment fully charged and ready to go.

Figure 10–10. LEGO pneumatic air gauge

Integrating Pneumatics with the NXT Robot

LEGO pneumatics are a great addition to LEGO robots because of their compact size and lightweight components. Compared to an NXT servo, the pneumatic actuators are quite light and can be added to your robot without causing much gain in weight. Also, because the actuators are relatively small, they can be installed in tight locations on your robot chassis, and the flexible hoses make the air lines easy to position.

LEGO pneumatics are also very strong. The amount of pressure you apply will determine how much force is applied by the actuator when it extends or contracts. You don't have to worry about gear slippage as you do with powered attachments, but you will need to be careful to not overpressurize your pneumatic components or else you could cause failure in one of the air hose connections and thus lose all your air pressure, making the pneumatic system useless.

When building a pneumatic attachment, you need to be aware of the distance the air switch is from the actuator. When the switch is close to the actuator, the cylinder will react faster than when the switch is a greater distance away. Because the air hose before the switch is full of pressurized air, and the hose coming out of the switch is empty, when the switch is triggered to open the air valve, the air must first fill the empty air hose before it can reach the actuator, thus making the response time slower.

Starting Out

There are two ways to fill your air tanks at an event: with a powered pump system or a manual pump system. The manual pump will be the more common approach at most events.

Some competitive LEGO robot teams will make use of an automatic pump system. To do so, they would need to use an NXT motor to run the pump, and this would defeat one of the advantages of using LEGO pneumatics on the robot. The idea is to increase the various ways to power an attachment, not really to swap one for another. This is not to say that automatic pump systems can't be done or won't be used; I'm just saying that using such a system will not be the common practice.

For a team that does not have any kind of powered pumping system, the robot's pneumatic systems will have to be filled with compressed air manually using the LEGO pump. This can be done in base or whenever the game rules allow the team to touch and handle the robot.

If your robot is going to be doing just a few minor things with the pneumatic attachment, a single full air tank should perform just fine, but if you think you're going to need a bit more air, adding multiple air tanks to your robot would be great option. Just remember that more tanks you have, the more time it's going to take to fill the tanks, and time is one of the things you won't have a lot of during most events.

Many teams will make the pneumatic attachment removable, so when its not being used, a teammate can pump up that air tank just before the attachment is installed on the robot and sent off to perform its mission. Don't try to fill the air tanks too early, because the LEGO pneumatic parts will leak a small bit of air. If you fill the tanks too soon, you might not get the full amount of pressure needed to complete your task.

You could also try to have multiple air tanks that you switch out when the robot returns to base. Doing so will require some nimble hands when attempting to connect the air hoses quickly.

Triggering the Attachment

Once your robot is pumped up and heading out to complete its task with the pneumatic attachment, how will you flip the switch to release the air needed to start the pneumatic action? Unfortunately, there is no easy answer to this question. In most cases, you will need to interact with an object on the field to flip the switch; very much like a touch sensor, the switch will have to be located in such a way that when the robot is in position, something on the field, or even the game table wall, will cause the air switch to flip and start the pneumatic process.

Many times, you will be able to just have the robot rub next to a field object or bump into something stationary on the game field. The amount of force needed to trigger the air switch is minimal, so you don't need to drive the robot fast or hit anything with a great deal of force; just a gentle tap is all that is needed.

Building Attachments

When building your pneumatic attachment, treat it the same way you would any other powered attachment. Make sure it's quick to take on and off of the robot chassis. Keep the actual attachment mechanism simple, and give lots of room for error when you can. Many of the same designs you can make for powered attachments can be made for pneumatic attachments as well, such as claws, lifts, and pushers.

Figure 10–11 shows an example of a lifting attachment that will connect to the DemoBot chassis. The attachment is all inclusive, meaning that the pump, air tank, switch, and of course, actuators are all part of the single attachment. This helps with quickly adding and removing the attachment. During an event, you will most likely not have time to connect and disconnect air hoses.

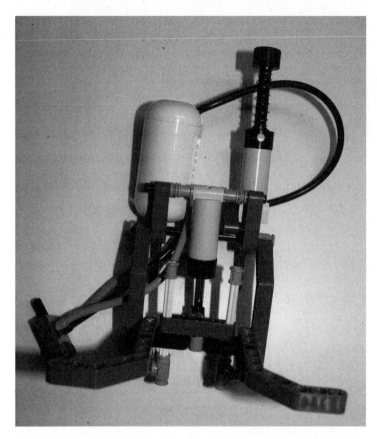

Figure 10–11. *A robot's lifting attachment using pneumatics*

Now, in Figure 10–12, the attachment is mounted on the DemoBot with a quick-release pin system, so the attachment simply drops into place. The air tank should have already been pumped up at this point, so it's just a matter of connecting the lift attachment and sending the robot out to perform its mission.

Figure 10–12. Demobot with pneumatic attachment connected.

Summary

LEGO pneumatics might not be necessary for most robot designs, but it's always a good idea to be aware that they are available. One time, you might find yourself needing an extra powered attachment that is lightweight and strong and can create linear movements. If you don't currently have any LEGO pneumatic parts available, I suggest that you at least invest in a few to give your team some hands-on experience with them. You'll be amazed at some of the creative ideas that can come from just hooking parts together and getting a better understanding of how they work.

PART 4

Programming

■ ■ ■

CHAPTER 11

Master Programs

A winning robot is more than just a fancy robot chassis with some cool attachments. Your robot's programs are essential to having a robot that will perform well at a competition. Most teams will develop a collection of programs to complete their missions. One of the biggest uses of time during a LEGO robotics event is the switching between each of these programs as the robot completes a mission. Even though the LEGO NXT brick provides a nice interface for switching between programs, it can be time consuming to search through the list of programs and select the right one for the next mission.

To speed up the process, you can select the necessary program with a *master program*, or a *sequencer*. The concept is that each of the programs for the missions is saved as a subprogram or My Block, as they're called in NXT. Next, you write a master program that will call each of the subprograms in the required order.

A simple master program will cycle through the programs one after another when each of the programs completes or a particular event has occurred, such as pressing touch sensor. Then, you can go to the other extreme and have a master program that not only advances automatically but allows for the user to navigate the list of programs and run a program out of order if needed. Master programs can be simple or complicated; it just depends on what your team needs and wants to do.

I would recommend having some form of a master program to help speed up the process for program selection; this can be a key factor in saving valuable time at an event. Also, having a master program can be one of the important programming items that judges look for during technical reviews. If you have developed a master program, be sure to point this out to your technical judges and be ready to explain how it works and why you have it.

My Blocks

For a master program to work, each of your mission programs need to be saved as an NXT-G My Block. My Blocks are really subprograms that can be accessed by other NXT-G programs. Don't worry about making your mission programs into My Blocks until you have the mission programs working as you desire. It's much easier to debug and test the programs when they are still just NXT-G programs and not subprograms. But don't worry; even after a program is converted to a My Block, you will be able to run it as an individual program for testing and debugging.

Defined Start and End Events

A key to writing mission programs that you intend to use in a master program is to make sure they have defined start and end events. The start event will just be the first thing in the program, so that part is easy and done when you created the program initially. However, teams don't always have a defined end event. Many times, teams will have the robot drive an unlimited amount of time when returning to base and depend on one of the team members to grab the robot when it crosses the base line and then stop the program with the controls on the NXT. In order for the program to work well in a master program, you do not want to press the stop button on the NXT brick, since this would actually stop your master program and not just the My Block that you're currently running. Instead, your program should end with an event from one of the sensors, such as touch sensor was pressed, or when a particular duration is met, such as number of motor rotations. This way, your program is not depending on someone to press the stop button on the NXT brick to end its execution.

Example Mission Code

The DemoBot has a Touch Sensor installed on the rear (see Figure 11–), so when the robot returns to base it can simply back into the wall of the table to let the program know that it has reached base. So once the Touch Sensor is pressed, the program knows to stop. Figure 11–2 shows an NXT-G program that runs a series of missions and then returns to base; once the wall is detected, the program will know it has reached base and allow the program to stop. A program such as this will make for a nice My Block.

Figure 11–1. DemoBot with rear facing touch sensor installed

Figure 11–2. NXT-G sample mission code

As noted in Chapter 3, be sure to add a Reset Motor block to the beginning of each subprogram. This will keep the different My Blocks from causing calculation issues with the NXT-G software tracking the rotations. Many times, when you switch from various subprograms that all have code relying on rotation calculations, the actual number of rotations can get out of sync, so having the Reset Motor block can prevent this from happening.

Simple Sequencer Program

The most common and easy-to-write master program is a simple sequence program. This master program will run the subprograms in a preprogrammed order. For most teams, a simple sequence program is a good start, and often, it will meet their needs. The drawbacks of such a program become apparent when something has to change on the fly. Say, for example, you need to rerun a subprogram that you already ran. If the master program offers the team no way to navigate through the programs, the user is forced to exit the master program and search for the subprogram using the standard NXT file menu system, thus costing valuable time.

Even though there are some limitations to a simple master program, it's a good place to start. Once your team has a good grasp of the purpose of such a program, you can continue to add new features such as program navigation, display options, and even program state memory. All of these concepts we'll talk about later when we cover more advance master programs in this chapter.

The Setup

Let's set up a situation in which a team may need a master program. For our example, the robot game has a series of nine missions the robot must complete in 2.5 minutes. The team has written five programs that will complete all these missions, which means some of the programs will handle more than one single mission. Combining programs is always good and is the first step in saving time. Whenever a team can combine missions into a single program this is a more efficient use of time and resources.

Now, in our example, the team will run its five programs in the same order each time it competes; a list of the names of the example programs that the team will run follows:

1. Collect Scientist Minifigs

2. Gather Core Sample & Stray Ball

3. Deliver Simple Machine & Scientist Minifigs

4. Deliver Car & Pallet of Power

5. Go to Final Parking Place & Deliver Package

■ **Note** When naming your programs it's always a good idea to give them a name that describes what the program does. Names like Program1 or MyProgram don't give the user an idea of what the program will actually do.

By looking at the list, you can see that some of the have to be run in a particular order. For example, the program called Collect Scientist Minifigs needs to run before Deliver Simple Machine & Scientist Minifigs, because we must collect the Scientist Minifigs before we can deliver them. Other programs might not be dependent of previous programs running, so their order is not as important. What is important is that you come up with an order and practice running the robot in that order over and over again. The robot returns to base when each of these programs is completed. Then, any new attachments are added, and the next program is selected so the robot can venture out again and attempt to complete the missions.

If you have worked with the NXT file menu system, you will have learned that the NXT puts the loaded programs in the order first in, last out (FILO). This means that, as you load your programs into the NXT brick, the very first program you load will always be the very last program run in the sequence as you navigate through the list of programs with the NXT file system navigation tools.

It can be very time consuming to have to flip though the programs each time the robot returns to base just to find the next program in your desired sequence. A simple sequencer program will resolve this issue and help you move forward quickly during a competition.

Creating My Blocks

One of the first things the team will need to do in our example is convert each of its programs into an NXT-G My Block. To do this, make sure each program has a defined end event, as we talked about earlier. None of the programs should depend on the user pressing the stop button on the NXT brick, since this will stop not only the My Block program but the master program as well.

To convert our programs into My Blocks, we simply select the entire program on the NXT-G programming screen, making sure all of the blocks and wires are selected—we don't want to leave out anything. Then, from the Edit menu, select Make a New My Block. Give your new My Block a name that will allow the user to understand what the My Block does without having to study the code too much. Ideally, a user should be able to just read the name of the My Block and have a good idea of the program's purpose. My Blocks also allow you to enter a description of what it does. I encourage you to write a brief description of the program to give other users a better idea of what is going on in the code.

Creating the Sequencer

Now that we have a My Block for each of the programs created and know the order in which we want to run those programs, we are ready to create a simple sequencer program to run them in order. In our NXT-G code, we will need a counter to keep track of where we are in the sequence of programs and a Switch block to switch between each of the programs. We will make use of the orange button on the top of the NXT brick as our trigger for switching between the programs. Every time the robot returns to base, one of the team members will simply press the orange button to increase the counter in our master program by one, and then the Switch block will use the value of the counter to know which My Block to run next. This process is much faster than having a team member navigate the NXT file system to find the next desired program; it also eliminates the possibility of selecting the wrong program.

Looking at the Code

Let's take a look at the code in Figure 11–3 in detail. In the beginning of our code, we set our counter to the value of 0. Even though we have five programs, they will be represented by the counter values 0 through 4. Since we are using a loop to rotate through the programs, we could use the counter value that is included with the Loop block, but later, when we build on to the program, having the Counter variable will be more useful.

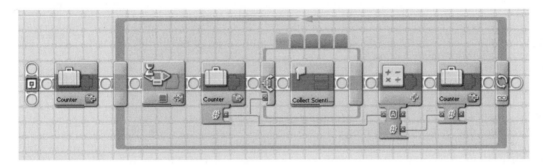

Figure 11–3. A simple sequencer master program

Once the program enters the Loop block, it will stop at a Wait block until the orange button on the NXT brick is pressed. When the orange button is pressed, the code will move to the Switch block, which will be connected to our Counter variable that executes whatever My Block we have associated with the counter sequence. Figure 11–3 shows that the My Block Collect Scientist Minifigs is in the first tab of the Switch Block. After the My Block in the Switch block is executed to completion, the Counter variable will be incremented by 1 by using the Math block. The new value will be saved back into the Counter variable.

This program will work as a master program, but what could we do to improve it? One of the first things it needs is the ability to offer some form of feedback to the user about what program is currently running and some kind of indication that the user has pressed the orange button. Feedback to the user is important so that it's obvious what the robot will attempt to do next.

In Figure 11–4, a Sound block was added after the Wait block, so when the orange button is pressed, a tone will sound to let the user know that the button press was received by the program. Also, you will notice that, before the Wait block, a Number to Text block was added to convert the value of the Counter to a text value so that it can be displayed on the NXT screen. This will allow the user to know where in the sequence process the block is currently.

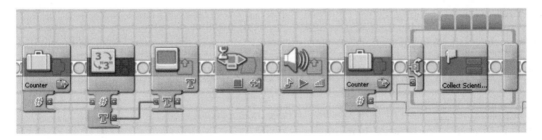

Figure 11–4. The simple sequencer with feedback to the user added such as tones and displays

Creating a Better Sequencer

As you saw with our simple sequencer master program, the concept is very straightforward: the master program runs a subprogram and waits for the user to tell it to run the next program in the correct order. The sequencer approach is great and a big time saver when trying to run a series of programs at a robotics competition. But what happens if you need to change things up at the last minute? What if you need to run the same program again before advancing to the next program? For example, in the first program, Collect Scientist Minifigs, maybe the robot missed collecting one the minifigs and you need them all for the second mission. You know if you run the program again, you might have a chance at collecting them, but your simple sequencer program has already advanced to the next program in your list. This is the case where having a few more advanced features in your program would be helpful, features such as program navigation.

Program Navigation

If you look back at the code we used for the simple sequencer master program, you can see that the value controlling what program runs is the Counter variable. If there was a way to increase or decrease the value of the Counter variable, we could have much more control over what programs are run in what sequence. In our example where we wanted to rerun the Collect Scientist Minifigs program, all we really need to do is get the value of the Counter variable back to 0, since this program is the first in our sequence. Figure 11–5 shows a new thread with a Wait block. This Wait Block is waiting for the left arrow button the NXT brick to be bumped. Using the bump, instead of pressed, setting is important because if we used the pressed action, the value would decrement continuously until the button is released. When the left arrow is bumped, the value of the Counter variable is decremented by 1. In our example, this would put us back at 0, where we want to be to rerun the first program in our sequence.

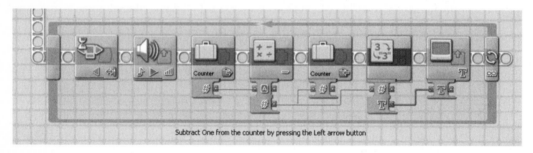

Subtract One from the counter by pressing the Left arrow button

Figure 11–5. NXT-G code to navigate to previous programs in the sequence

There is also a new Display block and Number to Text block added so that the user can see what order in the sequence is next. If we build on this concept, we can add a third thread for the right arrow button and allow the user to increment the Counter variable and move forward in the sequence of programs. Being able to skip forward would be useful if one of the programs needed to be skipped for example. Figure 11–6 shows the addition of the third thread to include the right button bump event.

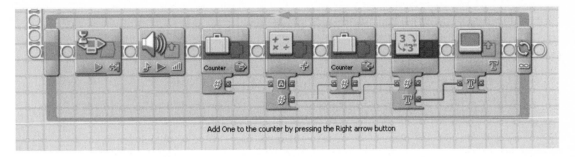

Figure 11-6. Navigation code to skip forward in the sequence

Sequence Rollover

One thing you might notice in the preceding code samples is that it wouldn't take long before our Counter variable exceeds the number of programs in our sequence or goes to a negative number. It would be wise for us to add some code to either prevent the Counter value from going below 0 or go higher than the number of programs we will actually need to run in our sequencer.

We can add a new My Block to our code that will handle the math for us and not allow the value to go out of range. In our example, the sequence range is 0 through 4. We are currently using Math blocks to increment or decrement our Counter value, so all we need to do is create a new My Block called SequenceMath block. The code would look like Figure 11-7.
The logic for this new program will be as follows:

1. Input current sequence value.

2. Input true or false if we are incrementing or decrementing the sequence value.

3. Assign, the current sequence value to the Sequence variable.

4. If we are incrementing, follow the true branch; otherwise, follow the false branch.

5. In the true branch, add 1 to the Sequence variable.

6. Check if the Sequence variable value is greater than the UpperLimit constant (which has a value of 4 in our example).

7. If the Sequence value is greater than the UpperLimit constant, assign the LowerLimit constant to the value of the Sequence variable.

8. In the false branch, subtract 1 from the Sequence variable.

9. Check if the Sequence variable is less than the LowerLimit constant (which has a value of 0 in our example).

10. If the Sequence value is less than the LowerLimit constant, assign the UpperLimit constant to the value of the Sequence variable.

11. Output the Sequence variable value.

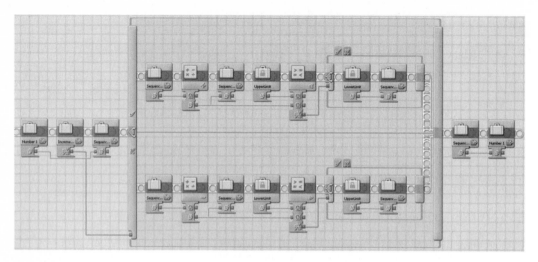

Figure 11–7. NXT-G program to cause the sequence counter to roll over if it falls out of range

If we follow the code along from the beginning (see Figure 11–8), we input two values in the Number 1 variable value: the current value of our Counter variable and the same value saved in the SequenceNumber variable. Next comes a logic variable called Increment. The Increment variable tells the program if we want to increase or decrease the value of our SequenceNumber variable. The reason we assign the Number 1 variable to the Sequence variable is so that, when we make it into a My Block, the Number 1 variable and the Increment variable will become input parameters for our new block.

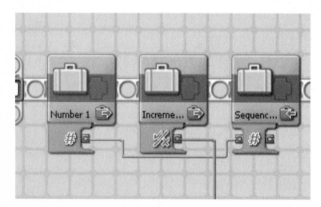

Figure 11–8. Setting up the input parameters

The Increment variable value is now passed to a Switch block, as shown in Figure 11–9. The true path will add 1 to the SequenceNumber value and the False path will subtract 1 from the SequenceNumber value.

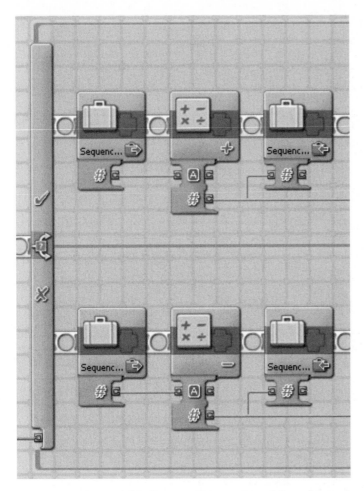

Figure 11–9. A Swtich block to test if we need to add or subtract from the sequence value

After the math on the SequenceNumber value is finished, another Switch Block will follow to see if we have exceeded our defined range of programs, as shown in Figure 11–10. This program has two constants defined: UpperLimit and LowerLimit. UpperLimit is defined as 4 for our example, and LowerLimit is defined as 0. Recall that the range for our example is 0 through 4.

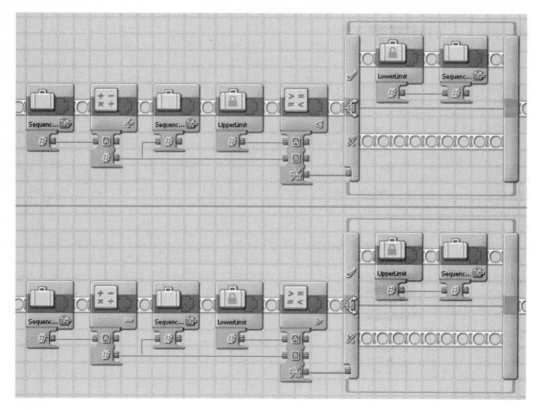

Figure 11–10. *Checking the new value of the Sequence variable to see if its out of range of our upper and lower limits*

If the Switch block finds that we have either exceeds or falls under the defined range value, we will simply reassign the SequenceNumber to the inverse limit value. For example, if our current SequenceNumber is 4 and we add 1 to it, SequenceNumber is now equal to 5. The value of 5 is outside the desired range, so we set SequenceNumber to the LowerLimit value of our range, 0. Now, SequenceNumber becomes 0. The opposite is true as well; if SequenceNumber falls below LowerLimit, the SequenceNumber will be reset to UpperLimit, which is 4.

Once we convert this program into a My Block called SequenceMath, the new My Block will have two input parameters, Increment (a true / false value) and the Sequence In (an integer), and one output parameter, Sequence Out. The input parameters are shown in Figure 11–11.

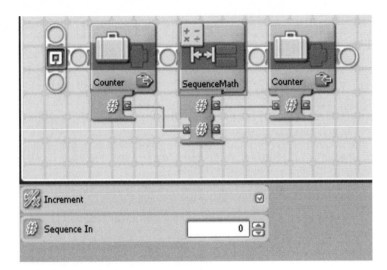

Figure 11–11. The SequenceMath My Block that was created from the code.

Now, we can replace the Math block in our current program with the new SequenceMath block; this will keep our program from placing our sequencer out of range. If the range changes for your programs, all that you need to do is adjust the UpperLimit constant in the SequenceMath block. Figure 11–12 shows the revised master program with these changes in place.

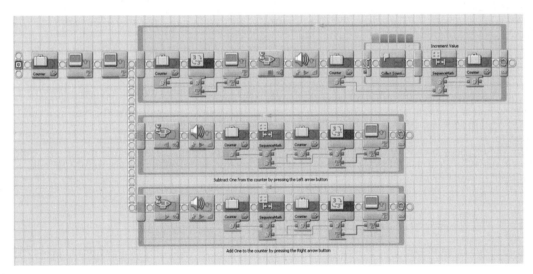

Figure 11–12. Revised master program with the new SequenceMath block included

You may find that you don't want the sequence to roll over when you get to the upper limit of your range and just simply stop incrementing beyond that value. To do this, you would just assign the value of the UpperLimit constant to your sequence when you reach the limit instead of the LowerLimit constant value.

Creating an Advanced Sequencer

The previous two versions of the sequencer will make great starting points for master programs. With very little effort, your team should be able to quickly add some nice user messages to the interface and perform well at any robotics event. If you want to add a little extra to your program, you could do something more advanced by adding some extra features to your program.

Program Display

The program displays the program sequence number on the NXT screen, and this is great if you have memorized the order of you programs and know that, when you see "0" on the screen, the Collect Scientist Minifigs program is running. But what if everyone on your team is not aware of this or what if you need to change the sequence and one of your team members forgets that "0" now equals the Deliver Car & Pallet of Power program? Relying on the program numbers can be confusing for people, and when you're running a robot under high pressure in a limited time frame, you want to make things as easy as possible.

The master program will be much user friendlier if we add a method that will display the program name instead of the program sequence number. You will notice that each of the code loops previously in this chapter uses a Number to Text block to convert the integer value of the sequence to a text value so that we can display the value on the NXT screen. What if we changed out the Number to Text block to a block that could convert the sequence number to a string value that told us the name of the actual program that is getting ready to run?

Figure 11–13 shows such a program. The variable called Sequence is passed into a Switch block that is very similar to the Switch block we have in the master program, but instead of having a My Block for each of our programs inside of it, there is a Text variable. Each sequence value will write a text value to the Text 1 variable, this text value is hard-coded, so if the order of the programs changes, this Switch Block will have to be changed just like the Switch block in the master program. The nice thing is that once we make this program into a My Block, you will only have to make the change to the code once, and it will update all locations in the master program where this My Block is used.

Now, the final step in the program is to write the value of the variable Text 1 to the text variable Program Name. The reason this step is done this way instead hard-coding the value into the text variable Program Name will become a bit more obvious when we convert this program into our new My Block.

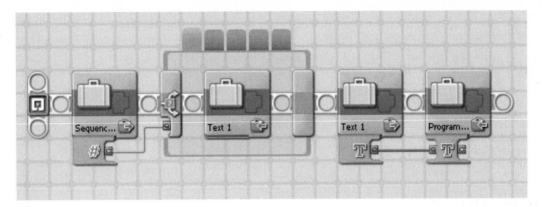

Figure 11–13. NXT-G program to retrieve the program name assocated with the given sequence number

So we have this nice little program and we want to make it into a handy Sequence to Program Name My Block. To do this right, we will select all the blocks in between the first variable block and the last variable block, but we won't include the first and last blocks, just as shown in Figure 11–14. By doing this, the new My Block will have an input parameter and an output parameter, as shown in Figure 11–15.

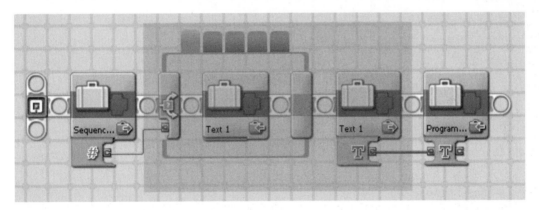

Figure 11–14. Code selection when making the new Sequence To Program Name My Block

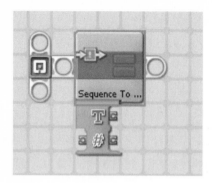

Figure 11–15. The Sequence to Program Name My Block

Now that we have our new Sequence to Program Name block, we can go back into our master program and replace the Number to Text blocks with our new block. Figure 11–16 shows what this would look like. The new block would be used in three places in our current master program.

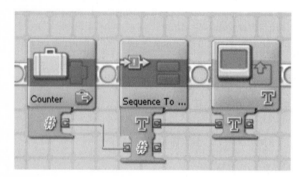

Figure 11–16. The Sequence to Program Name My Block in use

Saving State

Our master program is getting pretty advanced: it keeps our programs in order, has some smooth navigation features, and even displays the name of the program we're running (or about to run). What happens if the master program gets shut off on accident? When you start it up again, the sequence will start back at the beginning. This isn't too much of a crisis, since we can simply use our navigation buttons to move to the program that we wanted to run next. But what if, in all the confusion, you forget what program is next? Wouldn't it be nice if the NXT could remember where in the sequence it was before the master program stopped?

We refer to remembering our place in the sequence as *saving state*. We can keep a file on the NXT brick that stores the value of the current sequence order. Every time we change the sequence order, we update this file and write the value to the file, and every time the master program starts up, it can read this file and discover where it was last.

Figure 11–17 shows some sample NXT-G code that will read from a file when the program starts and pass the numeric value into our Number 1 variable. If the file does not exist on the system, the value of 0 is placed in the Number 1 variable. Now, the code will loop continuously with a wait for the NXT orange button press; this is similar to our sequencer code examples. Each time the orange NXT button is bumped, the variable Number 1 will be incremented by 1. Then, the file where we are saving our state value is deleted so that we can re-create the file by writing the new value to the file. Before the loop starts over, we close the file. The reading, writing, deleting, and closing are all done with the NXT File Access block.

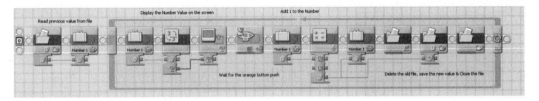

Figure 11–17. Sample NXT-G code for saving the state of a counter value

Adding logic such as this to the master program would not require much effort. It might not be necessary to do so, but if you find yourself needing to save the state of your sequence, a process such as this will work well.

Summary

A master program is not a requirement for any team, but most winning teams at the higher levels will have some type of master program. It not only gives teams an advantage in using time effectively, it shows the technical judges that your team understands advanced programming concepts. If you use such a program, be sure you understand why you're using it and how it works.

The examples I have shown in this chapter are strictly to get you started. There are many different ways to build successful master programs, so don't limit yourself to the ideas that have been given in this chapter. All of the examples given can be expanded into full-function sequencers with lots of nice, user-friendly messages and instructions for quick use.

CHAPTER 12

■ ■ ■

Program Management

Now, your winning robot is built, and you've started writing the programs to run it. How do you keep your NXT programs under control? When working as a team, everyone has their ideas of where the programs should be saved or how they should be named. What about when one team member needs to change another team member's code? How do you do keep track of who is making changes, and what if some code gets deleted that you later realize you needed to keep?

Also what about software upgrades and firmware upgrades? The NXT-G program is updated every so often, and it's important that your team work with the latest version. This is true for the firmware that your NXT brick runs as well. Keeping your robot's firmware updated is very important to make sure you avoid dealing with unnecessary software issues with your robot's programming.

NXT Updates

Having the latest firmware in your NXT brick is very important. New firmware is often available on the Internet, and it contains fixes for bugs and implements new algorithms for optimizing program space and execution.

■ **Note** *Firmware* is the software stored in the read-only memory of your NXT brick. The firmware is the software that tells the NXT how to behave and interact with the hardware and any loaded programs. For example, it tells the NXT how to display information on the screen or how to talk to a computer via the USB wire—things that you take for granted when using the NXT brick.

To download the latest drivers for NXT-G, you will need to install the NXT-G software onto your computer. When the application is loaded, from the Tools menu, select Update NXT Firmware, as shown in Figure 12–1. The resulting screen (see Figure 12–2) will display the current firmware versions available and allow you to connect with the Lego Education web site to check for more recent versions.

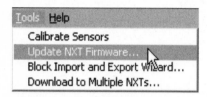

Figure 12–1. *The Update NXT Firmware menu item in NXT-G*

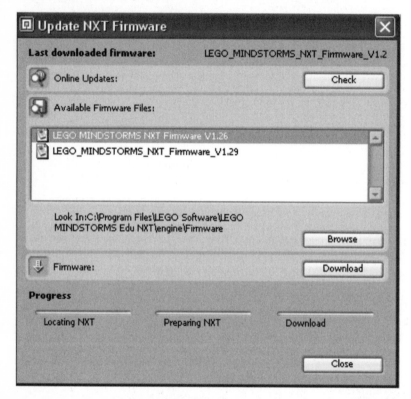

Figure 12–2. *The Update NXT Firmware dialog*

■ **Tip** It is always a good idea update firmware at the beginning of the season and stay with that update until you are finished, unless there is a known bug with that version of the firmware. Firmware updates have been known to change robot behavior, which can be devastating the day before the regional or state championship. In addition, if you use multiple robots, be sure all your robots have the same version of firmware.

The screen shown in Figure 12–2 shows two firmware updates that are already on your computer. Either they were downloaded it in the past or where installed with the NXT-G software.

To check to see if there is a later firmware update, do the following:

1. Make sure that you have an Internet connection.

2. Click the Check button in the Online Updates pane of the dialog.

The LEGO Education web page, shown in Figure 12–3, will be displayed. You may have to scroll down the web page to find the NXT Firmware version link with the highest version number. The version number is of the form X.Y.Z where "X" is the version, "Y" is the release, and "Z" is the point release. Version always takes precedence over release, which takes precedence over point release. So, version 2.0.0 is a higher version than 1.0.5 (which is higher than 1.0.4). The latest version is the one that you want to download.

If there are later firmware updates, download and unzip them into the engine\Firmware directory, where the LEGO NXT software is currently installed on your PC. Updates that you download will now show up in the Available Firmware Files pane.

To download an update to your NXT brick, do the following:

1. Connect your NXT brick to your computer.

2. Select the firmware file that you wish to send to the brick. (Usually, you will want the latest update).

3. Press the Download button.

Double check that the new firmware is loaded on the NXT brick by selecting Settings and then NXT Version. The FW value should display the current firmware version.

The LEGO Education Software Updates web site also contains updates for the NXT-G software as well. These updates happen less often than the firmware updates, but it's still a good idea to check every once in a while just to make sure you have the latest version.

Figure 12–3. LEGO Education Software Update web page

RoboLab Updates

If you decide to use RoboLab to program your robot, you will need to make sure it's updated as well by installing the latest firmware and software versions. These can be found on the www.LEGOEngineering.com web site, or you can have the RoboLab software check for updates automatically.

RoboLab and NXT-G use different firmware, which is the reason you cannot mix RoboLab programs and NXT-G programs on the same NXT brick. The MINDSTORMS NXT brick comes configured with firmware for NXT-G, so you must, therefore, download new firmware specific to RoboLab before you can begin programming your brick using the RoboLab language.

When you start the RoboLab program, there will be a menu item labeled Administrator on the main screen, as shown in Figure 12–4

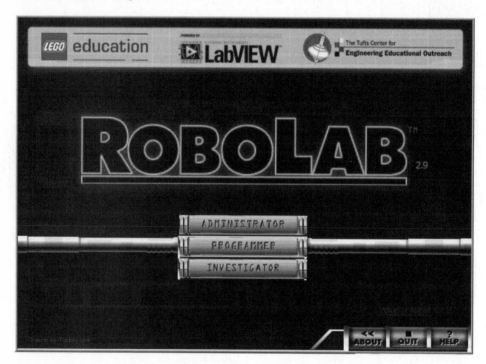

Figure 12–4. RoboLab main menu screen

Figure 12–5 shows the RoboLab Administrator screen, where you have the option to download the latest firmware to your NXT brick. When you click the Download Firmware button, the RoboLab software will check the Internet for the latest version of the firmware, and you will receive a prompt shown seen in Figure 12–6 if you need to update your NXT brick's firmware.

Figure 12–5. RoboLab Administrator menu

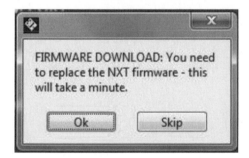

Figure 12–6. Firmware update dialog

Selecting OK causes RoboLab to install the most recent copy of the firmware to your NXT brick. Transmitting the firmware to your NXT brick may take a few minutes. Once the RoboLab firmware is installed on your NXT brick, you will not be able to use NXT-G programs on the NXT brick until you reinstall the NXT-G firmware on that brick. Again, only one type of firmware can be on the NXT brick at one time, either RoboLab or NXT-G.

Managing Source Code

Writing code for your robot as a team can become a challenge at times. Whether the team shares a single computer for writing the programs or has a computer for each team member to do programming, there can still be challenges for keeping the code under control.

Single Computer

If you're team is sharing a single computer for the robot programming, code management isn't as big a challenge as long as team members communicate. It's good to have a program task master, someone who keeps track of the changes and tries to keep the code safe. What I mean by "safe" is keeping it backed up. Nothing is worse than having a working program that then gets changed by someone else so that it no longer works as expected. When this happens, it's nice to have a copy of the previous, working version of the program.

Maintaining a backup copy would be the job of the program task master. Other duties would be to manage who works on what programs, be the gate keeper of the programs, and try to avoid unnecessary changes to programs. Many times, a person will change a program thinking something is wrong without realizing that they are setting up the robot incorrectly or using the wrong attachment. So the program task master needs to be familiar with all the code changes and able to discuss them with the team before any changes are made.

It's a good idea to back up programs after each team meeting. The programs, by default, are saved in the My Documents folder for the current user. For example, on my compute the path is

```
C:\Documents and Settings\jtrobaugh\My Documents\LEGO Creations\MINDSTORMS
Projects\Profiles\Default
```

Similarly, all of your My Blocks are saved under the following sort of path:

```
C:\Documents and Settings\jtrobaugh\My Documents\LEGO Creations\MINDSTORMS
Projects\Profiles\Default\Blocks
```

When backups are made of all the programs, both the \Default folder and the \Blocks folder should be backed up together, but you should keep the programs in their original folders. Many teams will keep a flash drive where they can copy the \Default folder at the end of each meeting, and they rename the copied folder using the current date, as shown in Figure 12–7.

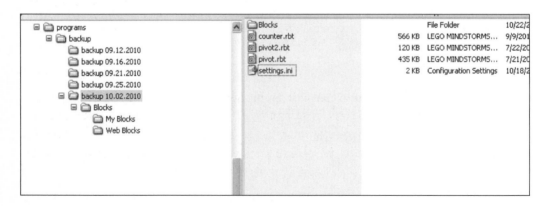

Figure 12–7. Backups of NXT-G programs

If you need to restore a previous program, you simply copy the file from the backup flash drive to the original location. Do not try to open the program directly from the flash drive; always work with your program in the default location. Otherwise, you will have corrupted the backup copy. Also, make backups of your files from outside of the NXT-G program editor; do not try to use the Save As method to copy the file to a different location. This can cause problems with your My Blocks linking properly in your program.

Network of Shared Computers

If you have multiple computers with different team members working on different programs at the same time, it might be helpful to have all the computers to use a single, shared network location for saving the programs. To do this, you will have to put in some extra effort to be sure that everything stays in sync.

The biggest concern is the location of your My Blocks. Even if you save your program to a location other than the default one, the My Blocks are still referenced from the system default location. For example, say team member Amy writes a program on her computer and it includes a reference to a My Block called AddToCounter. She saves the program to the shared drive on the network. Now, Ian opens the program that Amy wrote, but he doesn't have the My Block called AddToCounter on his computer, so his program will look like Figure 12–8 (the My Block will be displayed as broken).

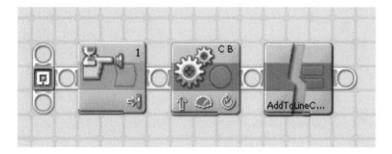

Figure 12–8. NXT-G program with broken My Block

The reason for the broken block is because the NXT-G program is looking at the Data Directory for the AddToCounter My Block, and that Data Directory is pointing to the local C drive of Ian's computer. The Data Directory is configured in the `settings.ini` file on each computer in the `My Documents\LEGO Creations\MINDSTORMS Projects\Profiles\Default` folder. If you want all the machines to use the same shared path, the Data Directory value on each machine must be changed.

■ **Caution** If you store all the files on a shared network location, consider this: When you go to your competition, most likely, you will not have any kind of network access; only in very rare situations would you have access to your shared network drive back at your school or home. If you need to access your programs at the competition, you will need to move copies of them locally to the computer you take with you to the event, and you will have to modify the `settings.ini` file to point to the local location and no longer the network location.

Flash Drives

Another common suggestion for teams is to store their programs on flash drives. The idea is that each team member will have his or her own flash drive to save programs. Each flash drive is mapped to the same drive path on the computer, so no matter who plugs up a drive, the Data Directory path in the `settings.ini` file is the same. Keeping the `settings.ini` file correct is very important, or you can run into issues with the broken My Blocks, as you saw in Figure 12–8.

For example if my Data Directory path is configured for the X drive, all my flash drives should also be mapped as the X drive on any computer they are connected. This can be done via the Computer Management application in Windows; it will allow you to specify the drive letter you wish to assign to your flash drive.

Also, with such a system, it's wise to have a master flash drive that your program task master uses to store the latest version of all the programs, in addition to the flash drives for team members. This would be the flash drive that you take with you to your competitions. To learn more about this method of program management, I suggest visiting the `www.TechBrick.com` web site; it has a very good write up on how to use such a system.

■ **Note** Be careful that you don't lose your flash drives. Keep them in a safe location when not in use. It's also still a good idea to make nightly backups of your programs.

File Naming

When working with your NXT-G programs, it's tempting to give the programs silly names, such as Liz Grabber Thingy, or encrypted acronyms, such as LGT. These names may be meaningful to the original programmer, but other people on the team are not going to have any idea of what they mean or do.

A team should come up with some standard naming conventions. Since the file name is what gets shown on the NXT brick screen, don't make it too long or too confusing. The name should say what the program does; having a noun and action can be helpful. Something such as GrabRings is a good start, but if you have multiple rings on the table, this name isn't all that helpful. Changing it to something like GrabRedRings could be much more useful. Now, someone reading that file name will be able to figure out what the program does quickly without having to dig too far into the actual code itself. If you have combined multiple tasks into a single mission, you can name the programs based on the mission names, for example, ZoneOneMission or DeliverGoodsMission.

Try not to include details such as the order in which the program is going to be run. Names such as FirstProgram or ProgramTwo are not helpful at all, because the order in which you run the programs could change, and these names really don't tell the operator what the program is designed to do.

Adding a version number is also a helpful idea when you're trying to keep track of your programs. If you have multiple programs in your folder, as shown in Figure 12–9, by looking at the file name, you can see there are two programs named PushCarToBase 1.0 and PushCarToBase 1.1. In that case, you can tell right away what the program does and which one is the newest version.

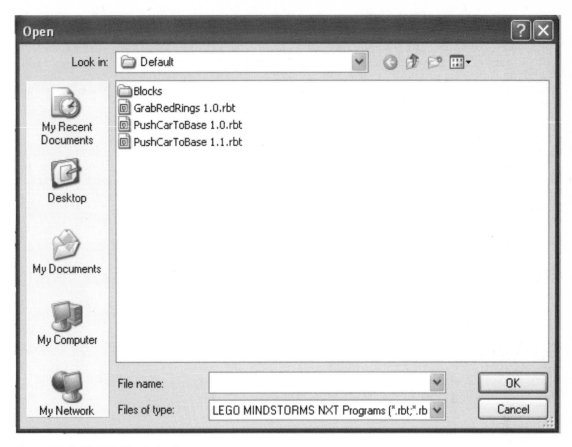

Figure 12–9. NXT-G file dialog box

Summary

Proper program management is critical in having a winning robot team. Even though the actual robot design and programs are important, without keeping your programs in order, your team can quickly get disorganized and fall behind. It's important to practice good code management skills from the beginning: make sure you're using you're using the latest versions of the code; keep files backed up, and use proper naming conventions.

CHAPTER 13

■■■

Documentation and Presentation

Part of operating a winning robot is being able to explain your robot to the technical judges. If your team cannot explain how and why the robot does what it does, you have missed the point of LEGO robotics. The actual robot performance is only a small part of a robotics competition; the most important component is what a team learns from the process. This is what the technical judges want to hear. They need to see and believe that the robot team actually did the work on the robot and learned something in the process.

Your team's job is to present to them in such a way that they understand everything you learned and the thought process you followed to get there. This is accomplished by documenting the journey your team followed to get a winning robot. Not only will detailed documentation help you impress the judges but it will also help your team keep a record of all the work you have done during the season.

Program Documentation

Keeping track of programs is always a struggle for teams. It's easy to just write the code, test it, and then move forward. While you're writing your programs, it's easy to remember what they do, but after a few weeks, keeping track of what each program does is a bit harder. So it is important to document the programs while their logic is still fresh in your mind.

This documentation will also help when other team members need to make changes or just understand what each program is doing when they are working on the robot. Having all team members familiar with the programs is important even if every person was not involved with programming a particular mission or task of the robot.

Program Description

One of the easiest ways to document your program is to add descriptive comments as you write the code. In NXT-G, it's simple to add these comments in each program using the Comment tool in the NXT-G software. The Comment tool is accessed in the NXT-G tool bar with the cartoon bubble shape shown in Figure 13–1.

Figure 13–1. NXT-G's commenting tool

When you select the Comment tool, your mouse cursor will change from an arrow to a text selector. Just move the pointer anywhere in your program and click the mouse to set the starting point for your text. Once your text is completed, you can switch back to the Pointer tool and relocate the newly typed text if necessary. The text you created will become another object in your code window that you can move and organize as needed.

Look at the code in Figure 13–2, without reviewing each code block, you would have a hard time understanding what is happening in this code. Even the original author of the code will quickly forget the details of what is happening in this code. Now, compare that to Figure 13–3. See how much easier it is to understand the code when there are comments present? You don't even have to understand what each of the NXT-G blocks does to get a quick understanding of the logic flow in this program.

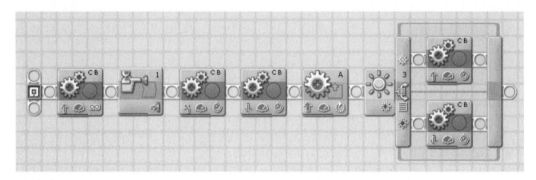

Figure 13–2. With uncommented NXT-G code, the flow is hard to understand.

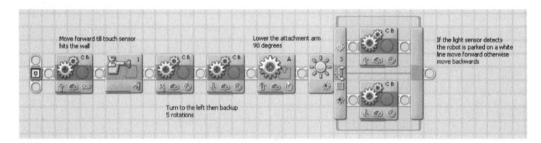

Figure 13–3. Commented NXT-G code is much easier to follow.

Using My Blocks with good descriptive names is also important when documenting the code, as shown in Figure 13–4. My Blocks that have descriptive names serve as self-documenting code. Of course, there is nothing wrong with having well named My Blocks and good comments too.

Figure 13–4. My Blocks with descriptive names help self-document the code.

The goal is to allow anyone, the author of the code or others, to read the code and quickly grasp what the purpose of the code is intended to do. The more you can add to help yourself and other users the better. However, be careful not to get too carried away. If the comments become too long and drawn out, other people will not want to read them. Keep your comments precise and to the point. If you feel you need further explanation of your code, you can always include that in a separate document.

Printed Copies of Programs

Having printed copies of your programs is always a good idea for any team. The printed versions of your code can serve as a failsafe backup if you lose all electronic versions of your code, and if you print your programs often, you will have a nice history of changes that were made to the programs if you ever need to go back and reference some older logic. Be warned that printouts do not show the settings in each of your program blocks, just the flow itself. So re-creating a program just from printouts alone will not be an easy task unless you have noted the setting for each block within your comments. But having the printed flow can be helpful in getting started again if necessary; hopefully, it will not come down to that for your team. Remember to back up your code on a regular basis.

Having a team technical notebook is a great idea; this will be a place where you can keep printed copies of your robot design and programs. Not only will be this be useful when talking to the technical judges but it will help your team keep such documents organized in a single location.

You should update your technical notebook with recent copies of your programs after you have made any notable changes. Be sure to date the printed copies as well, so you will know which version is the most recent. I would not throw away the older printouts right away, but you may want to move them to a different location in your notebook or a different notebook altogether. It never hurts to have too much documentation; you never know when you'll need to refer to it.

As you can see by the NXT-G Print dialog in Figure 13–5, you will be given multiple options of how you want to print your code.

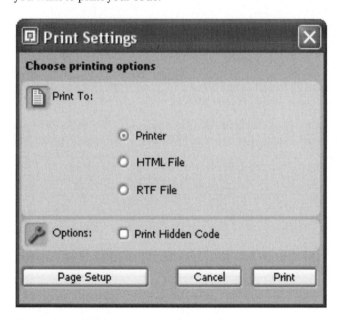

Figure 13–5. NXT-G printer settings dialog

Printing directly to a printer that your computer is connected to be often the simplest way to get a printed copy of your programs. By clicking the Page Setup button, you have the ability to adjust the margins and the options to include file details with the "Print header" option enabled, as shown in Figure 13–6. Things such as program name, modified date, and even a description (if one was saved with the program) will be included. Note that the program will be printed to fit the page size, so larger programs are going to be much harder to read, since the code blocks will be printed smaller.

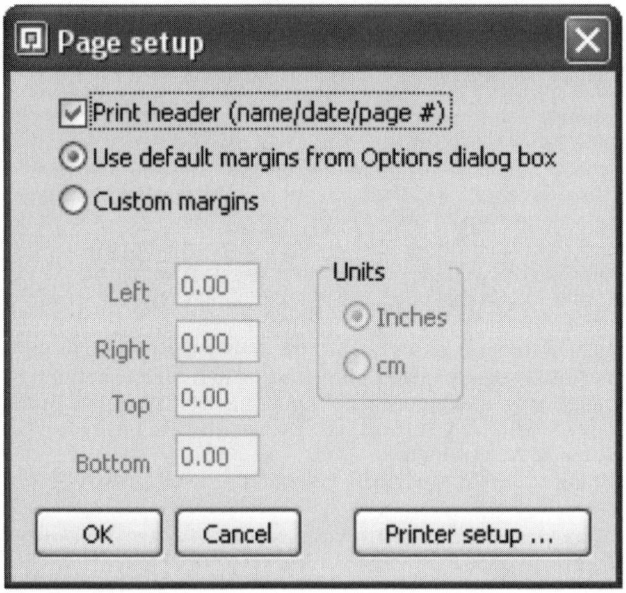

Figure 13–6. NXT-G page settings dialog

The Print Hidden Code option also shown in Figure 13–5 will allow for any code that is normally hidden from view in a block such as a Switch Block to be printed as well. So a single program could have multiple code sections printed on a single page. Figure 13–7 shows an example of a program printed to a page with both the Print Hidden Code and "Print header" options enabled.

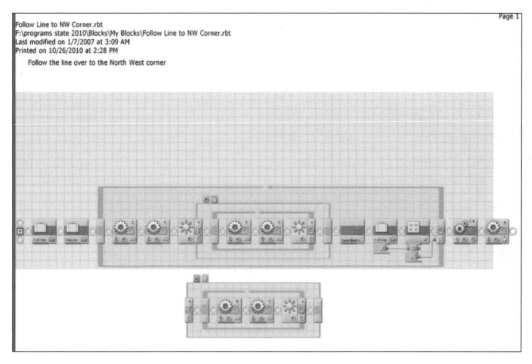

Follow Line to NW Corner.rbt
F:\programs state 2010\Blocks\My Blocks\Follow Line to NW Corner.rbt
Last modified on 1/7/2007 at 3:09 AM
Printed on 10/26/2010 at 2:28 PM

Follow the line over to the North West corner

Figure 13–7 Example of NXT-G program printed with the Print Hidden Code and "Print header" options enabled

You also have the option to print to an RTF (rich text format) file that can be opened by such programs as Microsoft Word; this is helpful if you wish to include copies of your programs in a more-inclusive document or a presentation document, such as a Microsoft PowerPoint slideshow. As with the Print To Printer option, both the Print Hidden Code and "Print header" options will work when you print to an RTF file.

If you choose to print to an HTML file, the NXT-G printer program will create multiple files for each image presented on the document, as well as an HTML file that can be viewed via a web browser. This feature is helpful if you want to present your program code to users on the Internet or an internal network. Even if you choose to not use the created HTML, having your code in individual images can be helpful for including sections of it in other documents. Figure 13–8 shows the same program as Figure 13–7 but in a web browser format instead. Figure 13–9 shows the list of files that were generated by the NXT-G program when using the HTML file feature for printing.

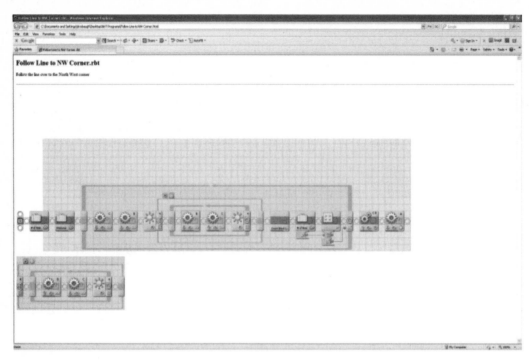

Figure 13–8 An NXT-G program printed to an HTML file

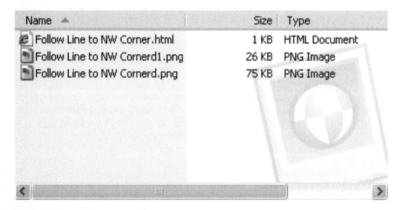

Figure 13–9. The list of files created by the NXT-G program when printing to an HTML file

Robot Design Documentation

Having documentation of your robot design can be just as important as having documentation of your code. Design documentation of your robot can aid in your presenting and explaining your robot to others.

How you create your documentation depends on how much effort and time your team has available. There are a variety of free LEGO CAD (computer aided design) applications available on the Internet. Many of the diagrams and instructions in this book were done with software available from the LDraw.org web site. This web site contains not only a variety of design programs but lots of instructional documents to help you get started with re-creating your LEGO robot virtually.

Creating your team's robot virtually with a CAD program might not be something you have the time or patience to do. If not, taking detailed pictures is also a great way to record your robot's design. And of course, there is no harm in having both CAD documents and photographs.

■ **Tip** No matter how you decide to make record of your robot design, be sure to include the resulting documents in your team's technical notebook.

Documenting Chassis Design

Unless you have the resources to build a back up robot, having design documentation of your robot can be very helpful if something happens to your actual robot. Few things are worse than being at a competition and finding a spare part in the box that you used to transported your robot to the event and not knowing where it belongs on the robot. Even worse is if the robot gets dropped (yes, it happens) and falls into pieces, and you don't know how to put those pieces back together again. Having some form of images or instructions for your robot can become critical at this point.

Also, it's a good idea to document the evolution of your robot design as it progresses during the season. This is helpful if you need to revert to a previous design. Also, technical judges like to see this evolution process of your design. Be prepared to describe the changes you made and why you made them to the judges as well.

If you choose to take photographs of your robot chassis, make sure to get pictures from various points of view. Having just a picture of the robot's profile will not be very helpful if you have to remember how the gears on the underside drive system are connected. In Figure 13–10, you can see some example photos that were used in a technical notebook to describe a robot's design.

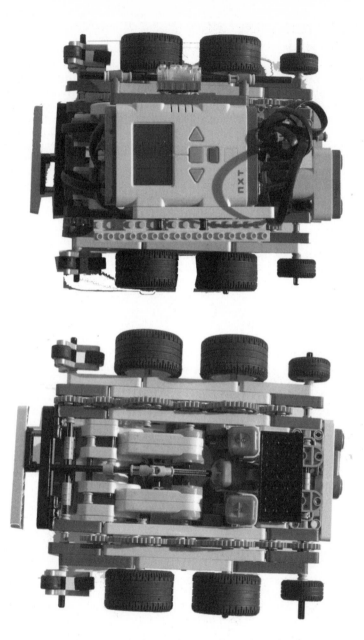

Figure 13–10. Photos of a robot design to be used in a technical notebook

Attachment Design and Description

Documenting the attachments your robot will use during the competition is also important. Again, having photos or CAD images of your attachments is helpful if you need to repair or replicate an attachment. Documentation will also help the team remember what task the different attachments are designed to perform, so besides just documenting the design of the attachments, including a description of what each attachment does, as well as what missions it will be used with, can also be a good idea.

Making a reference to what programs make use of an attachment can also be helpful. For example, you might have a program called DeliverBallsToBase that makes use of a cage attachment that your team built. On the page where you describe the cage attachment, you should note that the DeliverBallsToBase program requires this attachment. At the same time, you can make a reference to this attachment in your code documentation.

Presenting to the Technical Judges

Your documentation of the robot is not only helpful for keeping things in order for your team but for the technical judges as well. At most LEGO robotics events, your team will have to meet with a set of technical judges and explain to them what your robot does and why it does it. Most likely, you will have to demonstrate your robot as well. Having a technical notebook to document your team's progress over the season will not only keep the process fresh in your team members' minds but will help the judges see the effort your team put into the project.

Describing Your Solution Process

The technical judges are going to see a lot of robots in one day, so your team needs to make your robot stand out. What separates your robot from the others might not be the actual performance but the way you present it to the judges. Highlight the strong points of your robot. Talk about things you learned as a team while building the robot. Don't be afraid to mention failed attempts at missions and what you learned from your failures. The judges are just as interested in what your team learned as they are in the actual robot performance.

The team will need to be able to describe the process it followed to come up with its robot solution. At the beginning of this book, we talked about how to brainstorm robot chassis ideas and to work as a team to come up with a final design. Telling the judges of this process shows them that the design was a team effort and an original idea. Having some of these notes in your technical notebook can be helpful in remembering the process your team went through to get to your design. The judges may find some of your alternative designs interesting as well, so be prepared to share about them if asked.

Presenting Your Technical Notebook

A technical notebook is a good way to keep your design process organized and maintain a record of your team's work. How you organize you notebook is up to your team. Some teams prefer to categorize each section by task or mission for the challenge. Others may break it into software and hardware. How you choose to organize isn't important as long as you have some system for keeping your notes.

Some of the things that are typically included in a technical notebook follow:

- Robot design notes

- Mission lists broken out by tasks

- Diagrams or pictures of your robot

- Images of your attachments and their uses
- Printed copies of your programs
- Practice run score sheets

Really, anything that you believe would be helpful when explaining your robot and the design steps you followed to get where you are will be good to include in your notebook. Don't go crazy and overload it with unnecessary items, or else the important items might get overlooked.

Talking to the Judges

Judges will conduct the interview process differently at almost every event. Some are going to expect a scripted presentation, and others will just want to ask your team questions. Be prepared for both situations. My advice to teams is have a set of talking points ready, things that you would tell to teacher or friend if they asked about your robot. What are some of the things that make your robot unique or the experience building it special to you? By having these talking points, you can use them to give a presentation to the judges if necessary. If a presentation is not needed, you will be able to use these points to help answer the questions that a judge asks of the team.

Reviewing and doing practice judging is a great way for your team to prepare for a technical interview. Have someone besides your coach ask you questions, maybe a parent or teacher. I have even asked other team coaches do mock interviews with my team, as I did the same for theirs. The more practice a team has with answering questions and talking about its robot, the more confident the team will be with speaking about it.

Also, don't rely on one or two team members to answer all the questions. Everyone on the team should take part in the interview process. If team members are asked a question they don't know the answer to, it's OK for them to offer what information they do have and defer to another team member for further explanation. Everyone on the team is not expected to be the expert in every aspect of the robot.

In most team dynamics, some people will have more of a programming role and others more of a design role. The key is for everyone to understand what the robot does and have a basic understanding of the process. Have your stronger programming, and design, team members run through their contributions with all the team members, so that everyone feels confident talking about the robot and programs to some level.

When your team is talking to the judges, be sure to not talk over each other. If one team member is talking, don't interrupt even if you believe that person said something wrong. You may restate something a team member said about a question, but don't point out that someone didn't know the right answer to the question.

Speak clearly and with confidence. Try to avoid things like "umm" and "ahh" or just being silent. Be direct, and don't go into too much detail about topics unless the judges ask for more details. Often, your time with the judges is limited, so you want to cover as much about your robot as possible and not get stuck on one particular feature.

Summary

Having a winning robot is a multistep process involving good design, good programming, and proper organization. Keep notes at your meetings, and document the process as your team moves forward though the season. Having such documentation will show not only the hard work that went into the robot project but will assure judges that your team truly did the work and learned from the experience. Any team with good documentation will find that the presentation of their work is made much easier.

■ ■ ■

Building DemoBot

The instructions that follow show how to build the DemoBot robot used in many of the examples in this book. The instructions are presented step by step, in visual form. Each image shows a progression in the build and includes a callout box showing the additional pieces that you need for that particular step.

Assembling the Left-side Wheels

The following steps show how to build the left-side wheel assembly.

Left-Side Submodel One

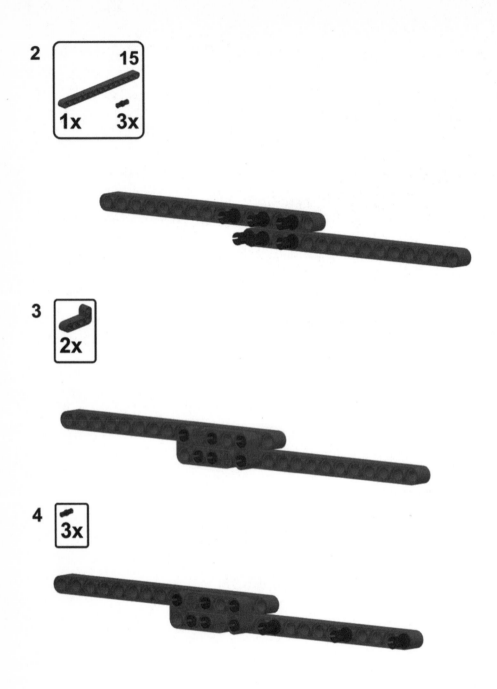

5 9

1x

Left-Side Submodel Two

1 15

1x

1x

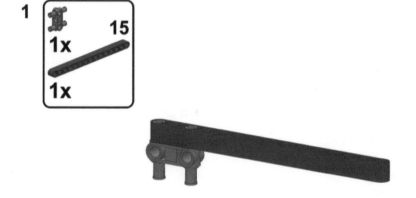

2

2x

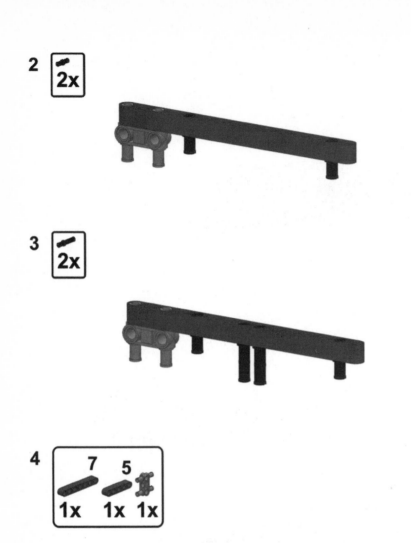

3

2x

4

7   5

1x   1x   1x

5

7

1x   2x

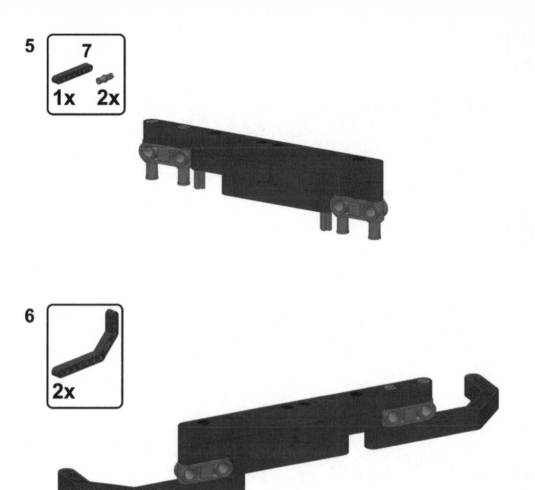

6

2x

7

10

1x   1x

8

8

1x   1x

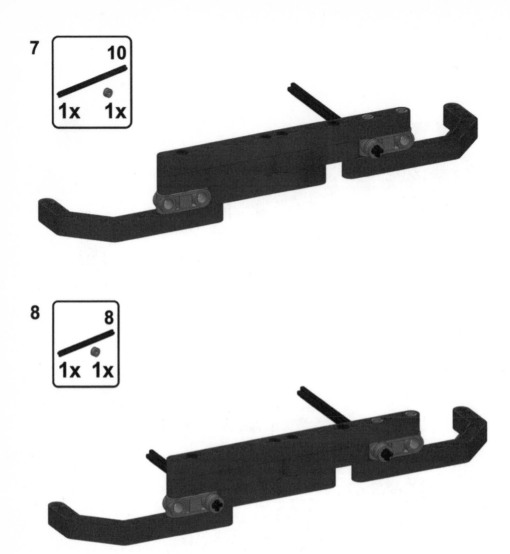

9

2x

10

1x 2x

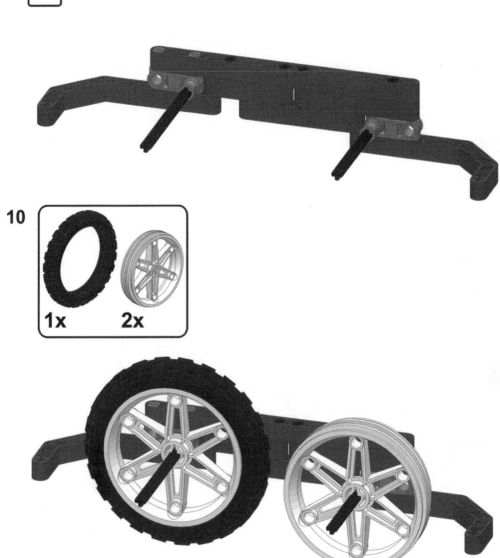

11

12

13

14

15 1x

Left-Side Main Assembly

1

2

3

4 `1x`

5

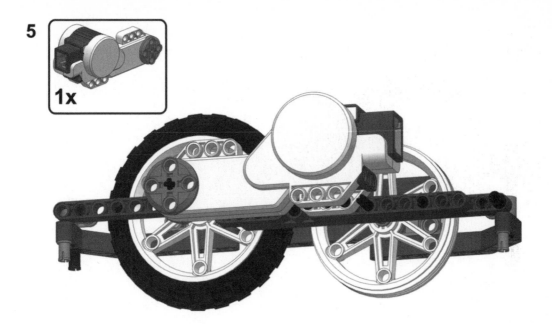

Assembling the Right-Side Wheels

The following steps show how to build the right-side wheel assembly.

Right-Side Submodel One

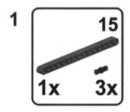

2

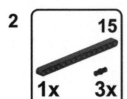

15

1x   3x

3

2x

4

5

Right-Side Submodel Two

1

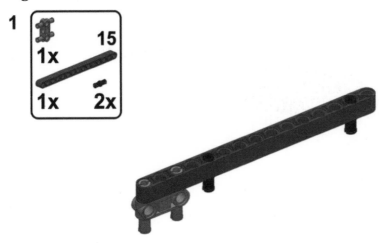

2

3

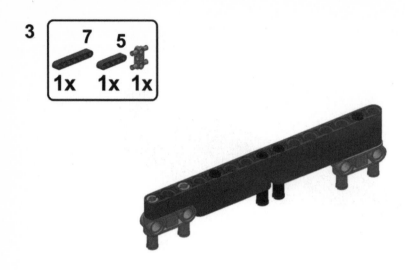

4

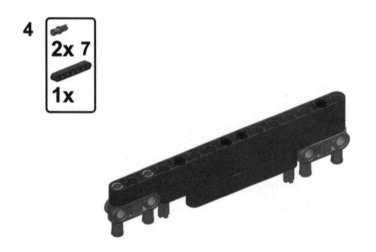

5

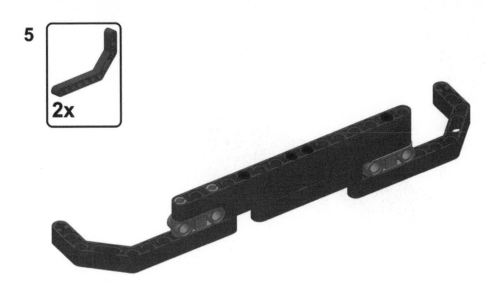

6

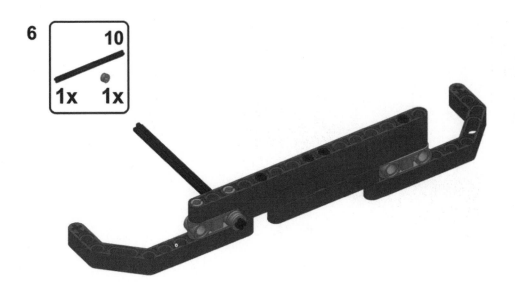

7

8
1x 1x

8

2x

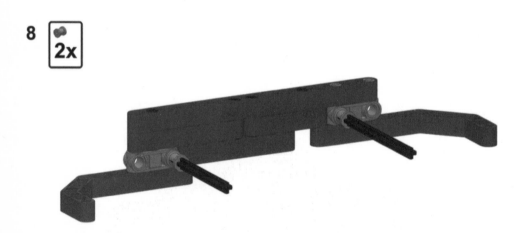

9

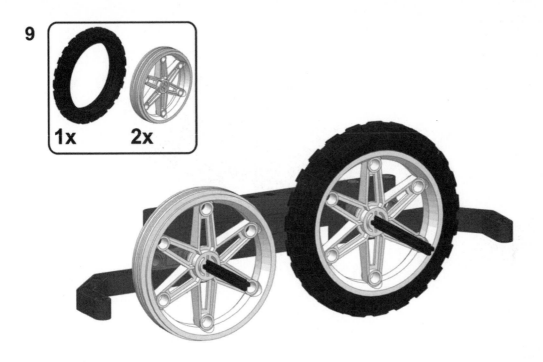

10

2x

11 2x

12 2x

13 2x

14 1x

15 **2x**

16

17 2x

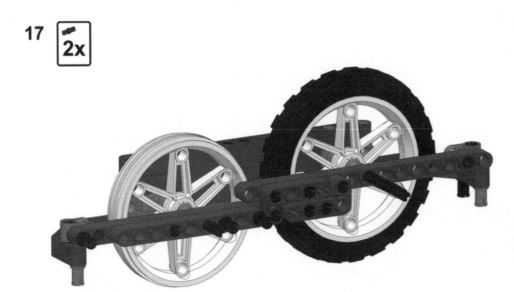

18 1x

19

1x

Assembling DemoBot

Here, we put the two wheel assemblies together to create our DemoBot.

1

2

3

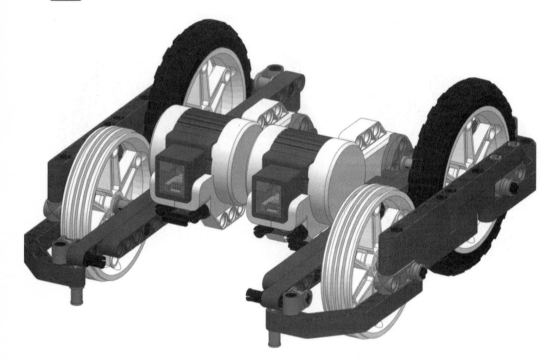

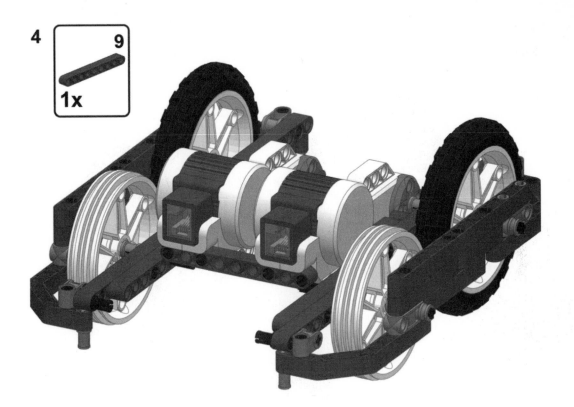

5

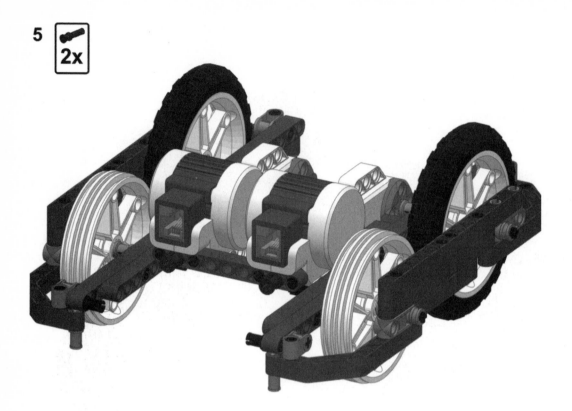

6

2x

7 2x

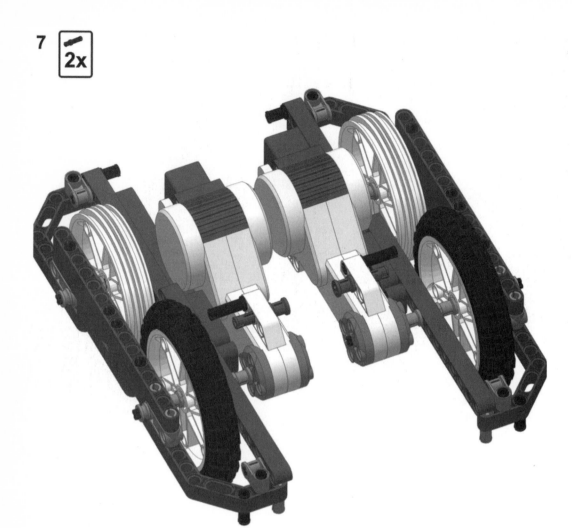

8

3

2x

9 2x

10

2x

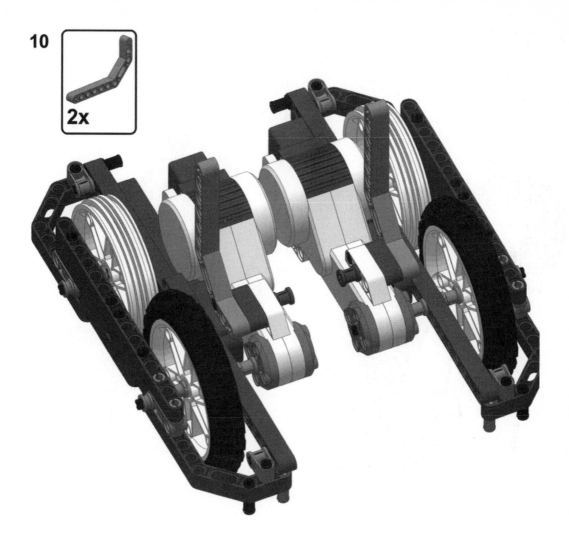

11

7

2x

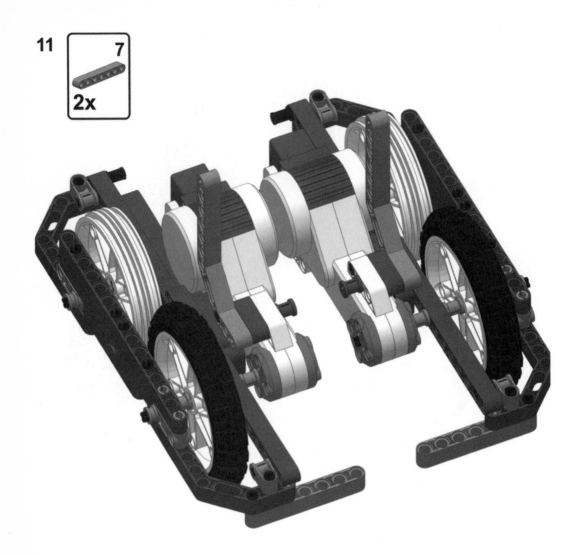

12 4x

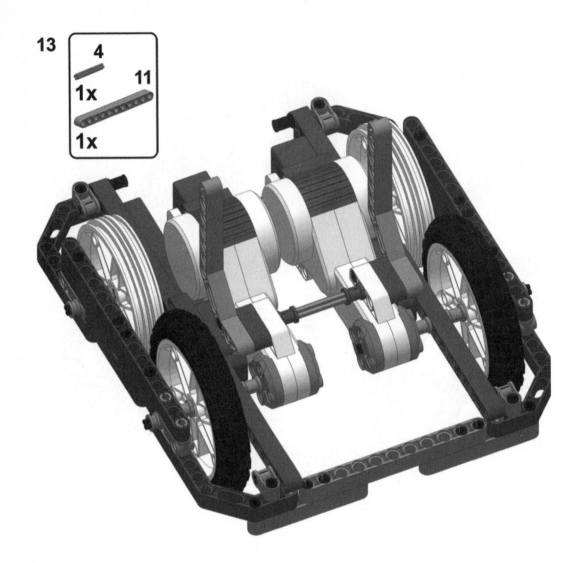

14

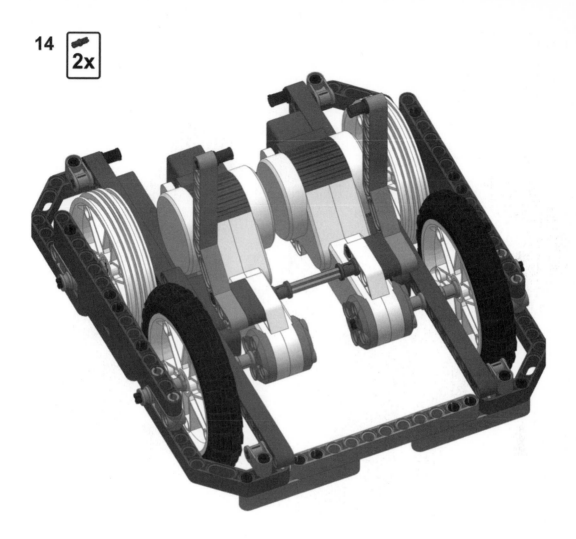

15 2x

16

15

1x

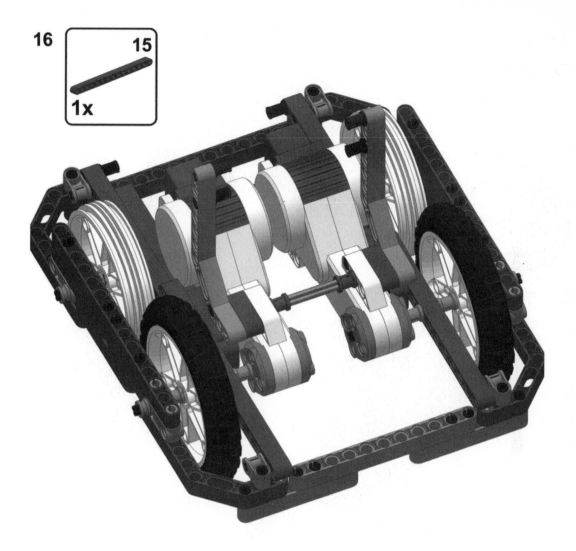

17

1x

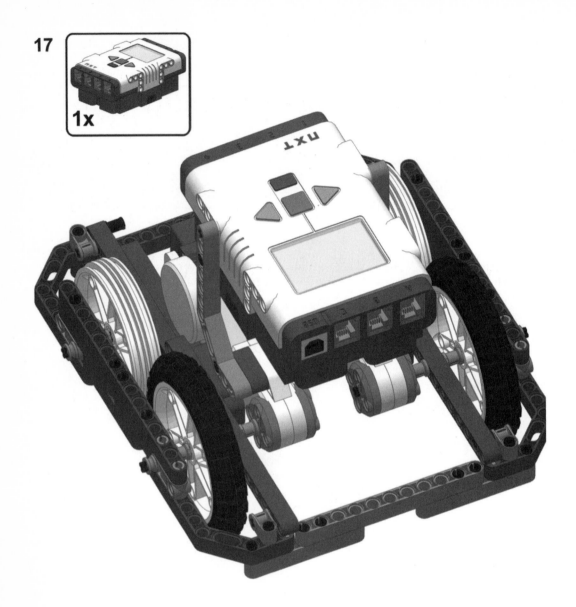

Building the Motor Matching Machine

These instructions will guide you in building the motor matching machine that was used in chapter 3 of this book. The machine is used to compare two NXT motors to find a pair of motors that are well suited to be used together. These instructions will guide you in building the motor matching machine step by step.

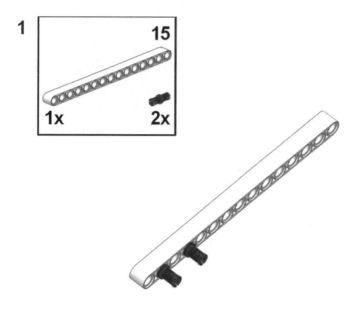

2

1x

3

2x

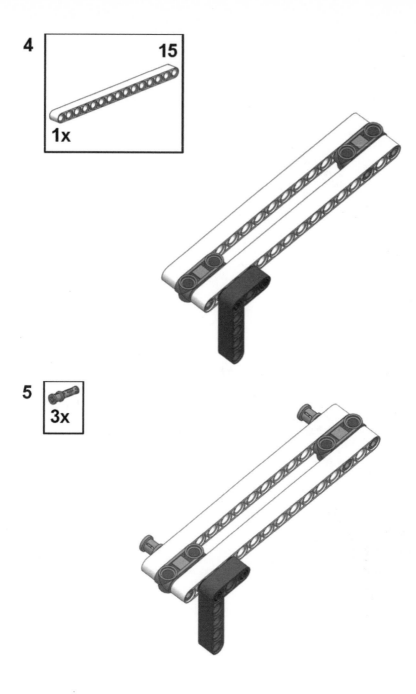

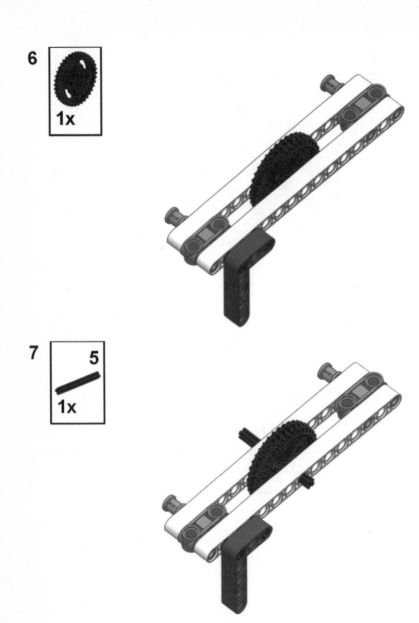

8

1x

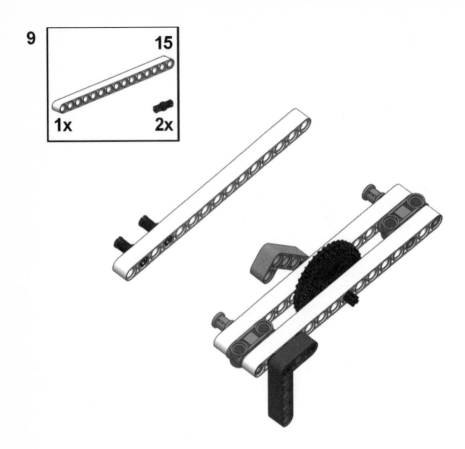

10

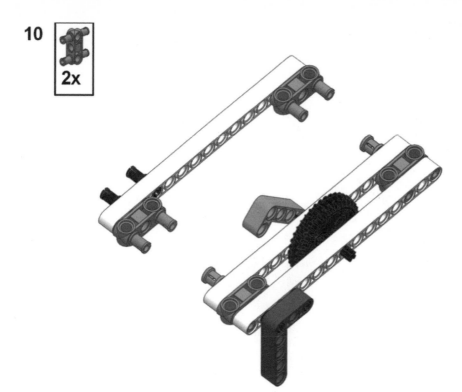

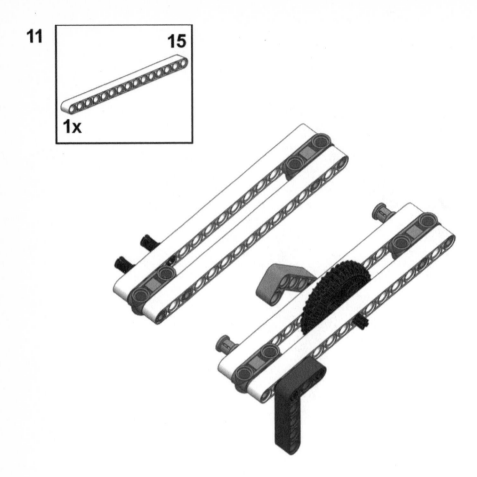

12

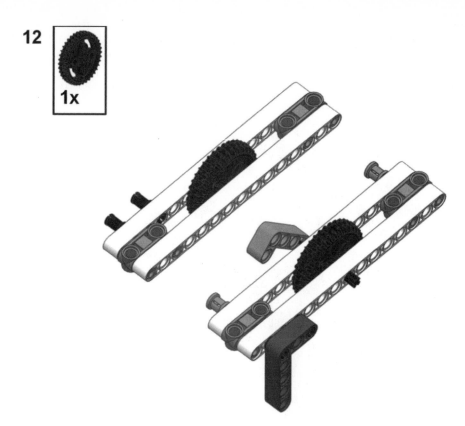

1x

13

5

1x

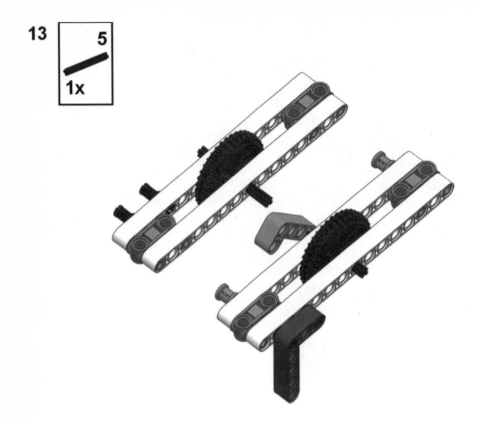

14

2x

15

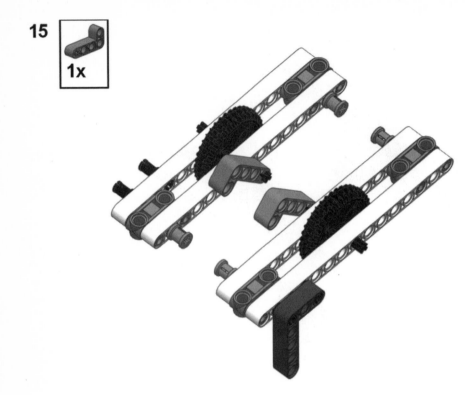

16

4

2x

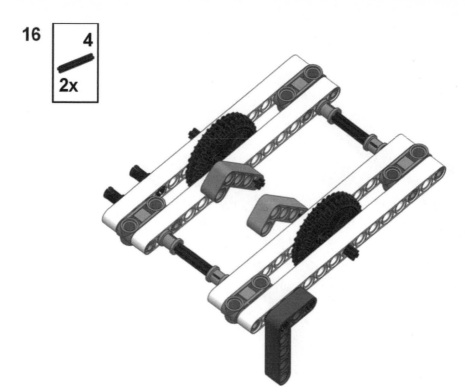

17

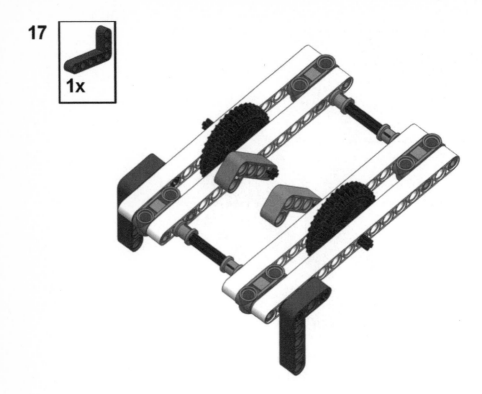

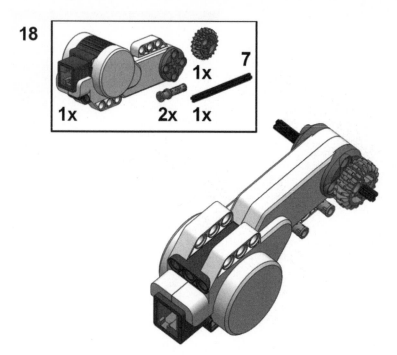

19

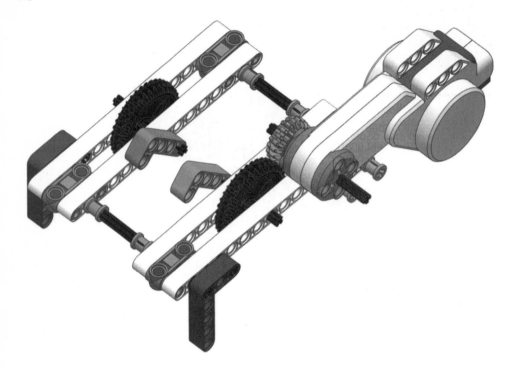

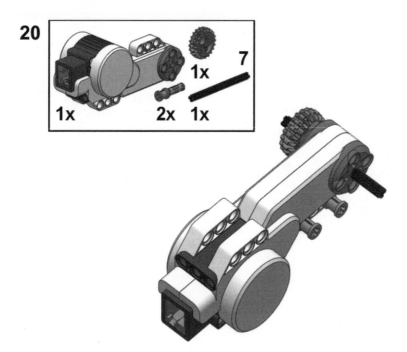

21

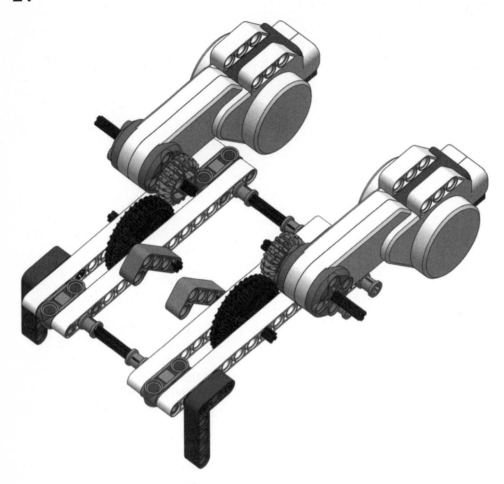

Index

■■■

■ Symbols and Numerics

You Need the Companion eBook

Your purchase of this book entitles you to buy the companion PDF-version eBook for only $10. Take the weightless companion with you anywhere.

We believe this Apress title will prove so indispensable that you'll want to carry it with you everywhere, which is why we are offering the companion eBook (in PDF format) for $10 to customers who purchase this book now. Convenient and fully searchable, the PDF version of any content-rich, page-heavy Apress book makes a valuable addition to your programming library. You can easily find and copy code—or perform examples by quickly toggling between instructions and the application. Even simultaneously tackling a donut, diet soda, and complex code becomes simplified with hands-free eBooks!

Once you purchase your book, getting the $10 companion eBook is simple:

❶ Visit **www.apress.com/promo/tendollars/**.

❷ Complete a basic registration form to receive a randomly generated question about this title.

❸ Answer the question correctly in 60 seconds, and you will receive a promotional code to redeem for the $10.00 eBook.

THE EXPERT'S VOICE™

233 Spring Street, New York, NY 10013